ENTANGLED GRIDLOCK

Entangled Gridlock

UNRAVELING POLITICAL STALEMATE AND ALLEVIATING HUMAN SUFFERING

Olivia K

Mohammed Altaf Hussain

Contents

1

Table of Content

Introduction

Chapter 1: The Landscape of Political Stalemate

1.1 Overview of the current political climate and the prevalence of gridlock.

1.2 Historical context of political stalemates and their impact on societies.

1.3 Examination of key factors contributing to the current state of political deadlock.

Chapter 2: The Human Toll

2.1 Exploration of the various ways in which political stalemate affects the lives of ordinary people.

2.2 Highlighting specific instances of human suffering linked to political inaction.

2.3 Analysis of the social, economic, and health consequences of prolonged political gridlock.

Chapter 3: Root Causes and Structural Issues

3.1 In-depth examination of the underlying causes of political stalemate.

3.2 Discussion on structural issues within political systems that contribute to deadlock.

3.3 Examination of partisan polarization, ideological rigidity, and other factors hindering effective governance.

Chapter 4: The Role of Political Leadership

4.1 Analysis of the impact of political leadership on breaking or perpetuating stalemate.

4.2 Leaders who successfully navigated through political challenges.

4.3 Exploration of the qualities and strategies necessary for effective leadership in overcoming gridlock.

Chapter 5: Global Perspectives on Political Stalemate

5.1 Comparative analysis of political stalemates in different regions of the world.

5.2 Examination of successful models for resolving political gridlock in various countries.

5.3 Lessons that can be learned from international experiences in addressing political challenges

.

Chapter 6: Mobilizing for Change

6.1 Exploration of grassroots movements and citizen initiatives that have successfully challenged political stalemate.

6.2 Analysis of the role of civil society in pressuring political leaders to act.

6.3 Strategies for mobilizing public support and fostering civic engagement to break the deadlock.

Chapter 7: Charting a Path Forward

7.1 Proposals for political and institutional reforms to mitigate gridlock.

7.2 Successful policy changes that have addressed root causes of political stalemate.

7.3 Vision for a more collaborative and effective political landscape, and the potential impact on alleviating human suffering.

7.4 Call to action for individuals, communities, and political leaders to work towards breaking the gridlock.

7.5 Vision for a future where political processes contribute to the well-being of society rather than perpetuating human suffering.

2

Introduction

In the complicated embroidery of human social orders, the entwining strings of legislative issues and administration assume a crucial part in forming the predeterminations of countries and people the same. However, as we stand at the junction of the 21st 100 years, we wind up caught in a snare of political impasse, where the cog wheels of administration appear to come to a standstill, leaving the general population in a condition of ceaseless vulnerability and disorder. "Caught Gridlock: Disentangling Political Impasse and Mitigating Human Misery" looks to unwind the complexities of this contemporary issue, investigating the extensive outcomes of political halt on the existences of ordinary individuals and testing the main drivers that have prompted such an unavoidable and apparently unmanageable circumstance.

Setting the Stage: The Scene of Political Impasse

As we leave on this excursion of understanding, giving occasion to feel qualms about our look the ongoing scene of political gridlock is basic. The lobbies of force, once proclaimed as strongholds of headway and navigation, have changed into fields of sectarian conflict and philosophical stalemate. The components intended to work with administration and protect the interests of the general population are currently shackled by the chains of polarization, delivering legislatures inadequate notwithstanding squeezing difficulties. This part digs into the overall patterns and elements that characterize the contemporary political environment, laying the preparation for an extensive investigation of the weaved connection between political impasse and human torment.

The Human Cost: Inadvertent blow-back of Political Impasse

In the shadow of political feebleness lies the obvious truth of human affliction. Section Two examines the diverse manners by which the gridlock in political apparatus resounds through the existences of standard residents. From financial difficulties to compromised medical services and stressed social texture, the human cost of political inaction is broad. Through impactful contextual investigations and true models, we reveal the stories of the people who endure the worst part of regulatory latency, revealing insight into the pressing requirement for a nuanced comprehension of the multifaceted associations between political choices and the government assistance of society.

Underlying drivers and Primary Issues: Unloading the Gridlock Puzzle

To take apart the conundrum of political gridlock, Part Three explores the maze of underlying drivers and primary issues that underlie the present status of undertakings. An investigation into the elements of sectarian polarization, philosophical unbending nature, and fundamental defects inside political establishments uncovers the mind boggling web that catches dynamic cycles. By disentangling these intricacies, we establish the groundwork for a more profound comprehension of the difficulties that impede compelling administration and sustain the impasse.

The Job of Political Administration: Exploring the Labyrinth

Political initiative stands as a reference point in the midst of emergency, equipped for directing countries through tempestuous waters or capitulating to the flows of friction. Part Four basically evaluates the effect of initiative on political gridlock, introducing contextual analyses of pioneers who have either effectively explored through difficulties or capitulated to the tensions of polarization. By analyzing the characteristics and techniques fundamental for successful administration in breaking the stop, we enlighten the expected pathways toward more responsive and dependable administration.

Worldwide Points of view on Political Impasse: A Relative Focal point

The fifth section broadens the extension, offering a relative investigation of political impasses across the globe. By comparing assorted encounters, we plan to recognize examples, victories, and disappointments in various districts. From parliamentary moves to grassroots developments, this section investigates the changed methodologies taken by countries to address political difficulties. The examples gathered from worldwide encounters give important experiences into possible methodologies for breaking the gridlock and proposition a worldwide viewpoint on the weaved idea of political choices and human government assistance.

Activating for Change: The Force of Common Society

Perceiving that change frequently starts at the grassroots level, Part Six looks at the job of common society in testing political impasse. From the perspective of grassroots developments, resident drives, and the preparation of public feeling, we disclose the potential for aggregate activity to impact political cycles. By featuring cases where urban commitment has compelled pioneers to act, we present techniques for preparing public help and encouraging a culture of dynamic citizenship that rises above the limitations of political gridlock.

Diagramming a Way ahead: Proposition for Change

In the penultimate part, we stand up to the subject of how to diagram a way ahead from the mess of political impasse. Proposition for political and institutional changes become the dominant focal point, tending to the main drivers recognized before in the account. Drawing from effective instances of strategy changes that have broken the gridlock in different settings, we imagine a future where administration isn't a wellspring of stagnation however an impetus for positive change.

Past Impasse, Toward Progress

As we close our investigation, the combination of bits of knowledge and discoveries from the first parts fills in as a compass highlighting a future unburdened by the shackles of political gridlock. The source of inspiration is clear: past the inactivity lies the potential for progress. By grasping the perplexing interchange between political choices and human misery, by disentangling the layers of gridlock that smother successful administration, we seek to make ready for an existence where political frameworks serve the prosperity of society as opposed to sustaining its misery. "Ensnared Gridlock" welcomes perusers to participate in this excursion of grasping, reflection, and promotion for a stronger and sympathetic worldwide local area.

Chapter 1

The Landscape of Political Stalemate

The Scene of Political Impasse: An Extensive Investigation

In the huge and unpredictable territory of current legislative issues, the scene is in many cases defaced by the tireless presence of political impasses. These stalemates, set apart by an absence of understanding or progress, have turned into a central trait of administration in different corners of the world. Grasping the roots, appearances, and results of political impasses is vital for exploring the complicated elements that shape the course of countries and impact the existences of residents.

At the core of political impasses lie well established philosophical contrasts. Whether established in verifiable complaints, social differences, or clashing dreams for the future, these philosophical partitions establish a climate where compromise turns out to be progressively subtle.

The conflict of convictions frequently leads to a condition of gridlock, where regulative bodies, chief branches, and, surprisingly, grassroots developments end up entrapped in a snare of contradicting points of view. This gridlock, while a characteristic result of different feelings in a majority rule society, becomes risky when it obstructs the capacity to resolve major problems and serve the aggregate government assistance.

One of the essential difficulties in exploring the scene of political impasse is the breakdown of viable correspondence. While contradicting groups become dug in their positions, discourse frequently lapses into a skirmish of manner of speaking, where the objective isn't common seeing yet rather the justification of one's own convictions. The disintegration of correspondence channels further extends the separation, making protected, closed off environments where contradicting voices are overwhelmed, and the potential for settling on some shared interest is seriously reduced.

The results of political impasses stretch out a long ways past the blessed lobbies of government foundations. At its center, an impasse mirrors an inability to sanction strategies that address the developing requirements of society. Whether it be financial changes, civil rights drives, or ecological guidelines, the stagnation brought about by political gridlock hampers progress and compounds existing difficulties. The repercussions are felt by the general population, as issues, for example, pay imbalance, medical care access, and environmental change stay ignored, propagating patterns of human misery.

The trapped gridlock in governmental issues frequently leads to a feeling of frustration among residents. As commitments go unfulfilled and basic issues wait without goal, trust in the political cycle disintegrates. This disintegration of trust is a destructive power that can sabotage the actual underpinnings of a majority rules system, as residents question the viability and authenticity of their chosen delegates. The subsequent pessimism can prompt separation from the political interaction, further sustaining a pattern of ineffectual administration.

To comprehend the scene of political impasse, looking at the job of institutional frameworks is fundamental. The plan of political frameworks, including balanced governance, partition of abilities, and electing processes, assumes a huge part in molding the elements of administration. While these instruments are planned to forestall the maltreatment of force, they can likewise add to the entrenchment of contradicting groups, making it challenging to accomplish agreement on pivotal issues. Changing these organizations to cultivate participation without compromising vote based standards is a fragile difficult exercise that requires cautious thought.

Additionally, the scene of political impasse isn't static yet advances in light of changing cultural elements. Moving socioeconomics, social changes, and mechanical progressions all add to the back and forth movement of political scenes. Adjusting administration designs to oblige these progressions is critical for forestalling drawn out gridlock and guaranteeing the political framework stays receptive to the necessities of a dynamic and various populace.

A basic part of understanding political impasses is perceiving the job of outside factors. International strains, financial tensions, and worldwide emergencies can all apply effect on the political scene of a country. These outer powers can either fuel existing divisions or act as impetuses for participation. Exploring the interchange between inward elements and outside pressures is fundamental for policymakers looking to break liberated from the shackles of gridlock and address the major problems confronting their social orders.

Tending to the scene of political impasse requires a complex methodology that envelops both primary changes and changes in political culture. One road for breaking the gridlock is cultivating a culture of discourse and split the difference. Empowering open correspondence, undivided attention, and a readiness to figure out some mutual interest can prepare for cooperative arrangements. Political pioneers, specifically, bear the obligation of establishing a vibe that values participation over conflict.

One more road for goal lies in rethinking the electing processes that shape political portrayal. Relative portrayal, positioned decision casting a ballot, and other option discretionary frameworks can offer a more nuanced impression of different sentiments inside society, diminishing the polarization that frequently prompts impasses. Furthermore, crusade finance change and measures to check the impact of exceptional interests can moderate the effect of cash on governmental issues, cultivating a more evenhanded and responsive political scene.

In equal, there is a squeezing need for institutional changes that smooth out dynamic cycles without compromising popularity based standards. The adequacy of administration structures relies upon their capacity to work with participation while forestalling the centralization of force. Finding some kind of harmony requires a cautious assessment of existing establishments and an eagerness to adjust them to the difficulties of the 21st hundred years.

Moreover, tending to the scene of political impasse requires a promise to straightforwardness and responsibility. Residents should approach precise data about the dynamic cycles, permitting them to consider their agents responsible for their activities. Embracing straightforwardness reinforces the vote based establishment as well as encourages trust between the administered and the overseeing.

Social and financial disparities frequently add to the propagation of political impasses. Tending to these incongruities requires designated strategies that inspire underestimated networks and make a more level battleground. Civil rights drives, instructive changes, and monetary strategies that focus on inclusivity can relieve the divisions that add to gridlock, encouraging a more impartial society.

Worldwide collaboration likewise assumes a vital part in exploring the scene of political impasse. In an interconnected world, worldwide difficulties, for example, environmental change, pandemics, and financial emergencies require cooperative arrangements. Strategy and participation between countries can rise above political partitions, encouraging a feeling of solidarity in resolving issues that rise above borders.

The scene of political impasse is a complicated landscape that requests a nuanced and complete methodology. By cultivating a culture of discourse, changing electing processes, adjusting institutional systems, advancing straightforwardness, tending to social imbalances, and encouraging global collaboration, social orders can explore the difficulties presented by political gridlock. This excursion requires an aggregate obligation to the standards of a majority rules system, the prosperity of residents, and the versatility of administration designs to the developing necessities of society.

The scene of political impasse is both an impression of cultural divisions and a chance for restoration. It is a source of inspiration for political pioneers, policymakers, and residents the same to rise above philosophical contrasts, embrace discourse, and work towards normal arrangements. Breaking liberated from the ensnared gridlock requires a deliberate work to reshape the political scene, cultivating a more responsive, impartial, and comprehensive administration that serves the aggregate government assistance of individuals.

1.1 Overview of the current political climate and the prevalence of gridlock.

Outline of the Ongoing Political Environment and the Pervasiveness of Gridlock: Exploring Difficulties in Contemporary Administration

As we stand at the junction of the 21st 100 years, the worldwide political scene is set apart by an intricate interaction of powers, belief systems, and difficulties that shape the course of countries. Understanding the ongoing political environment requires an exhaustive investigation of the variables adding to the commonness of gridlock — a peculiarity that has become progressively unavoidable and weighty in contemporary administration.

At the core of the ongoing political environment is a scene characterized by polarization. The philosophical gorge between political groups has broadened, establishing a climate where compromise is much of the time saw as an indication of shortcoming instead of a foundation of powerful administration. This developing gap is obvious in the way of talking of political talk, the polarization of news sources, and the developing propensity of people to fall in line with outrageous positions, practically ruling out the nuanced center ground where agreement can be manufactured.

The ascent of egalitarian developments and pioneers further highlights the enraptured idea of contemporary governmental issues. Fuelled by complaints, genuine or saw, these developments frequently gain by the dissatisfactions of disappointed populaces, promising extremist change and a break from the apparent disappointments of laid out political frameworks. While such developments can act as articulations of authentic worries, they likewise add to the entrenchment of contradicting philosophies, making the possibility of settling on something worth agreeing on progressively testing.

The disintegration of confidence in political foundations is an unavoidable subject in the ongoing political environment. Outrages, defilement, and a feeling of separation from the worries of the general population have prompted a decrease in trust in chosen delegates and government bodies. This disintegration of trust subverts the authenticity of popularity based processes as well as adds to the gridlock by encouraging an environment of incredulity and negativity that obstructs valuable exchange.

In the time of data, the job of media in molding popular assessment and impacting political talk couldn't possibly be more significant. The multiplication of web-based entertainment stages has democratized data spread however has additionally brought about protected, closed off environments where people are presented fundamentally to points of view that line up with their previous convictions. This peculiarity, known as tendency to look for predictable feedback, adds to the solidifying of philosophical positions and the polarization of general assessment, making it challenging to settle on some shared interest on antagonistic issues.

The pervasiveness of gridlock in contemporary governmental issues shows most apparently in the brokenness of regulative bodies. In parliamentary vote based systems and delegate republics the same, the corridors of government frequently reverberation with the sound of philosophical conflicts, prompting authoritative impasses, government closures, and the powerlessness to pass significant regulation. The effect of this gridlock reaches out past the offices of force, influencing the existences of residents who rely upon successful administration to resolve major problems.

A fundamental part of understanding the ongoing political environment and the pervasiveness of gridlock is perceiving the worldwide idea of these difficulties. In a time where countries are interconnected in terms of professional career, innovation, and shared difficulties, for example, environmental change and general wellbeing emergencies, the capacity to arrange worldwide reactions is central. In any case, international strains, patriot feelings, and contending interests frequently impede powerful cooperation on a worldwide scale, adding to a feeling of gridlock in resolving issues that rise above borders.

Monetary contemplations likewise assume a huge part in molding the ongoing political environment. Variations in riches and admittance to open doors have powered social agitation and political discontent in numerous social orders. The journey for monetary solidness and flourishing frequently outweighs everything else in political plans, prompting strategy gridlock as contending dreams for financial administration conflict. Besides, the effects of globalization, mechanization, and the developing idea of work present difficulties that request imaginative strategy arrangements — an errand made more troublesome by political idleness.

In the domain of homegrown governmental issues, the job of vested parties and campaigning can't be neglected. The impact of strong halls, addressing corporate interests, promotion gatherings, or specific enterprises, can influence the equilibrium of political navigation. While vested parties are a genuine piece of the popularity based process, their unbalanced impact can add to gridlock by hindering the section of regulation that might contradict their inclinations.

The commonness of gridlock is likewise obvious in the domain of international strategy, where the powerlessness to manufacture a bound together position on worldwide issues can have extensive outcomes. Conflicts over discretionary methodologies, exchange approaches, and security techniques can prompt a divided worldwide reaction, frustrating the capacity of the worldwide local area to successfully address shared difficulties.

Tending to the difficulties presented by the ongoing political environment and the pervasiveness of gridlock requires a multi-layered approach. One key component is cultivating a culture of useful discourse. Embracing open and conscious correspondence is fundamental for crossing over philosophical partitions and figuring out some shared interest on issues of public and worldwide importance. Political pioneers, specifically, bear the obligation of establishing a vibe that values coordinated effort over conflict, empowering a feeling of bipartisanship and collaboration.

Transforming electing processes is one more road for relieving the commonness of gridlock. Elective democratic frameworks, like positioned decision casting a ballot or corresponding portrayal, can offer more nuanced impressions of different conclusions inside society. Furthermore, resolving issues connected with crusade finance and campaigning guidelines is urgent for guaranteeing that the political scene isn't unduly impacted by strong vested parties.

Institutional changes are additionally basic for exploring the difficulties presented by gridlock. The plan of administration structures, including governing rules, should find some kind of harmony between forestalling the maltreatment of force and working with compelling independent direction. A cautious assessment of existing foundations, with an eye towards upgrading their flexibility and responsiveness, is fundamental for breaking the pattern of political impasse.

Straightforwardness and responsibility are essential standards in tending to the disintegration of confidence in political establishments. States should focus on straightforwardness in dynamic cycles, furnishing residents with admittance to exact data about approach decisions and the reasoning behind them. Responsibility measures, including systems for considering chose authorities liable for their activities, are fundamental for reestablishing confidence in the popularity based process.

Tending to financial incongruities is vital for diminishing social turmoil and political discontent. Arrangements that focus on comprehensive monetary development, impartial appropriation of assets, and admittance to open doors can assist with overcoming any issues between various fragments of society. Civil rights drives, schooling changes, and designated mediations to elevate underestimated networks are necessary parts of a thorough system to address the underlying drivers of gridlock.

Worldwide collaboration is basic even with worldwide difficulties. Discretion and coordinated effort between countries should rise above political partitions, cultivating a feeling of solidarity in resolving issues that influence the whole planet. Reinforcing global establishments and systems for coordination can improve the viability of worldwide reactions to shared difficulties, moderating the effect of gridlock on the world stage.

The ongoing political environment, described by polarization and the commonness of gridlock, presents the two difficulties and open doors for cultural reestablishment. Exploring these intricacies requires a promise to cultivating a culture of exchange, transforming discretionary cycles, adjusting institutional systems, advancing straightforwardness, tending to monetary differences, and encouraging worldwide participation. Breaking liberated from the ensnared snare of gridlock requests an aggregate work to reshape the political scene, guaranteeing that administration structures are responsive, impartial, and situated toward the aggregate government assistance of individuals. As we face the difficulties of the present, it is the obligation of residents, policymakers, and pioneers the same to diagram a course toward a more comprehensive, versatile, and viable type of administration that meets the developing necessities of a dynamic and interconnected world.

1.2 Historical context of political stalemates and their impact on societies.

The Verifiable Setting of Political Impasses and Their Effect on Social orders: Following the Strings of Gridlock Through Time

To fathom the contemporary difficulties presented by political impasses, one should set out on an excursion through the chronicles of history, where the strings of gridlock have woven themselves into the texture of different social orders. The foundations of political stalemate, set apart by an absence of agreement and participation, can be followed across various ages, revealing insight into the intricate elements that have molded the course of countries and impacted the direction of human social orders.

In old civilizations, the idea of political impasses finds reverberations in the battles for power and administration. The city-conditions of old Greece, for instance, wrestled with inward divisions that frequently prompted gridlock in direction. Contending political groups, like the leftists and oligarchs in Athens, competed for control, bringing about a teeter-totter of strategy changes and inversions. The failure to arrive at enduring arrangements prevented the improvement of durable administration designs and left these social orders helpless against outer dangers.

Also, the Roman Republic confronted difficulties related with political gridlock. The strain between the Senate and famous congregations, combined with the battles for control among contending officers, established a climate where agreement on crucial issues demonstrated tricky. The results of such gridlock were clear in the disintegration of the Roman Republic's vote based standards and the possible progress to majestic rule, denoting a groundbreaking second over Western political history.

Archaic Europe, in the midst of medieval designs and governments, saw epic showdowns that led to political gridlock. Medieval masters, competing for impact and independence, frequently opposed focal power, blocking the foundation of brought together administration. The Magna Carta in 1215, a basic report in the improvement of established standards, arose as a reaction to the gridlock between Lord John and his nobles, featuring the getting through strain between unified power and nearby independence.

The Renaissance and Illumination periods introduced novel thoughts regarding administration, yet political gridlock continued. The development of sacred governments looked to figure out some kind of harmony between imperial power and the freedoms of subjects. Nonetheless, the battle for power among rulers and parliamentary bodies, as found in Britain, exemplified the getting through difficulties in accomplishing an amicable connection between various parts of government.

The Time of Upheavals, from the American Upset to the French Insurgency, delivered yearnings for delegate administration. In spite of these groundbreaking minutes, political gridlock stayed a repetitive subject. In the US, the discussions over the design of the national government during the drafting of the Constitution reflected profound philosophical divisions. The trade off came to, however momentous, didn't altogether dispose of the seeds of future gridlock, as proven by ensuing struggles over issues like servitude and states' privileges.

The nineteenth century saw the spread of popularity based standards and the ascent of mass developments. Nonetheless, the mission for portrayal and interest didn't necessarily convert into compelling administration. European parliamentary frameworks, wrestling with class pressures and provincial variations, experienced times of political gridlock that hindered social and monetary changes.

The twentieth 100 years, set apart by worldwide contentions and philosophical battles, saw the effect of political impasses for a terrific scope. The interwar period, loaded with monetary difficulties and philosophical polarization, saw the ascent of dictator systems as a reaction to saw administration disappointments. The failure of majority rule governments to actually address cultural worries added to the disintegration of confidence in just organizations.

The post-The Second Great War period delivered new international elements, yet political gridlock persevered in both the East and the West. The Virus War competition between the US and the Soviet Association frequently prompted political stalemates and upset worldwide collaboration. In the mean time, in Western vote based systems, philosophical divisions over issues, for example, social liberties and the Vietnam War energized political polarization, adding to a feeling of gridlock.

In the last 50% of the twentieth hundred years and into the 21st 100 years, the elements of political impasses developed close by globalization and mechanical progressions. While the finish of the Virus War brought expects another period of participation, the intricacies of a globalized world introduced new difficulties. Monetary inconsistencies, ecological worries, and transnational issues requested cooperative arrangements, yet political gridlock at both the public and global levels frequently obstructed progress.

The effect of political impasses on social orders from the beginning of time has been complex and significant. One of the persevering through results is the disintegration of public confidence in political establishments. At the point when gridlock forestalls compelling navigation and obstructs the execution of approaches that address major problems, residents become disappointed with the vote based process. The disintegration of trust can prompt withdrawal, lack of concern, or, in outrageous cases, a dismissal of popularity based standards by and large.

Financial results additionally go with political impasses. Failure to pass spending plans, sanction financial changes, or address monetary difficulties can prompt financial stagnation and vulnerability. Financial backers, organizations, and shoppers might confront unsteadiness, impeding monetary development and worsening social disparities. The effects of such financial gridlock are felt most intensely by weak populaces, further adding to cultural abberations.

The social texture of a general public is woven with the strings of its administration structures. Political impasses can strain this texture, prompting social distress and polarization. At the point when issues like social equality, civil rights, or personality become caught in political gridlock, cultural divisions develop. The outcomes should be visible in developments for change, fights, and, now and again, social disturbance as residents try to break liberated from the shackles of inaction.

Ecological difficulties, including environmental change and asset consumption, present existential dangers that require composed worldwide reactions. Political gridlock on the global stage can hinder the execution of extensive arrangements. The results of ecological gridlock reach out past public boundaries, influencing the prosperity of networks and environments around the world.

Besides, political impasses can subvert the adequacy of establishments intended to safeguard basic liberties and advance harmony. Global associations, like the Unified Countries, may confront deterrents in answering contentions and helpful emergencies when international pressures lead to gridlock. The results are borne by those trapped in the crossfire, as tact vacillates and endeavors to address worldwide difficulties are hindered.

Breaking the pattern of political impasses requires a nuanced comprehension of verifiable examples and a guarantee to versatile administration. Gaining from the examples of the past, social orders can explore the intricacies of the present and fabricate an establishment for a stronger future. It includes reconsidering administration structures, cultivating a culture of joint effort and split the difference, and embracing creative ways to deal with critical thinking.

Changing discretionary cycles is a basic part of tending to verifiable examples of political gridlock. As social orders develop, so too should the systems through which people take part in the majority rule process. Elective democratic frameworks, crusade finance changes, and endeavors to upgrade the representativeness of chosen bodies can add to breaking the pattern of dug in political divisions.

Institutional changes are similarly fundamental for versatile administration. Analyzing the designs of government, the appropriation of abilities, and the components for independent direction can distinguish regions where changes are required. Finding some kind of harmony among balanced governance and the limit with respect to powerful administration requires persistent assessment and variation.

Straightforwardness and responsibility assume significant parts in remaking trust in political establishments. Open correspondence, available data, and components for considering pioneers responsible for their activities are central for reestablishing confidence in the popularity based process. Incorporating straightforwardness into dynamic cycles can demystify administration and encourage a feeling of divided liability between residents.

Additionally, addressing social and financial imbalances is basic to breaking the authentic examples of political impasses. Arrangements that advance inclusivity, equivalent admittance to open doors, and civil rights can alleviate the variables that add to cultural divisions. Training, monetary changes, and designated intercessions can inspire minimized networks and make a more evenhanded starting point for administration.

In the worldwide setting, it is fundamental to encourage global collaboration. Perceiving the interconnectedness of difficulties, for example, environmental change, pandemics, and monetary emergencies requires a promise to cooperative arrangements. Tact, exchange, and a common feeling of obligation can rise above verifiable international contentions, preparing for viable worldwide administration.

The verifiable setting of political impasses uncovers an embroidery woven with repeating designs and persevering through difficulties. Following the strings of gridlock through time enlightens the intricacies of administration and the significant effect of political stalemate on social orders. Breaking liberated from verifiable cycles requests a deliberate work to gain from the illustrations of the past, adjust administration designs to the necessities of the present, and encourage a culture of cooperation that rises above the divisions that have tormented social orders since the beginning of time. As we explore the difficulties of the 21st 100 years, the reverberations of history act as an aide, encouraging social orders to produce a way toward versatile administration, strength, and a reestablished obligation to the standards of a vote based system and the prosperity, everything being equal.

1.3 Examination of key factors contributing to the current state of political deadlock.

Assessment of Key Elements Adding to the Present status of Political Gridlock: Disentangling the Mind boggling Web

The present status of political stop is a multi-layered embroidery woven from different strings of intricacy, mirroring an intersection of verifiable, social, monetary, and institutional variables. To comprehend the foundations of the stalemates that incapacitate political frameworks across the globe, an extensive assessment is essential, digging into the complexities that add to the overarching gridlock.

One of the basic variables powering the present status of political stop is the heightening polarization of political belief systems. In numerous vote based systems, the extending hole among left and right, moderate and liberal, has arrived at extraordinary levels. This polarization isn't just apparent in that frame of mind of government yet in addition penetrates the more extensive cultural talk, forming general assessment and impacting citizen conduct. The entrenchment of political personalities adds to an "us up against them" mindset, where compromise turns into an apparent double-crossing as opposed to a sign of viable administration.

Media polarization assumes a critical part in enhancing and sustaining political divisions. The ascent of sectarian news sources, combined with the approach of virtual entertainment, has made closed quarters where people are presented fundamentally to data that lines up with their previous convictions. This peculiarity, known as "tendency to look for predictable feedback," supports existing viewpoints and upsets the capacity to participate in valuable discourse. Subsequently, residents are many times captivated in their political perspectives as well as in how they might interpret realities and reality, making it trying to settle on something worth agreeing on.

Institutional factors likewise contribute fundamentally to the present status of political stop. The plan of administration structures, including governing rules, division of abilities, and constituent frameworks, can either work with participation or compound gridlock. While these institutional instruments are expected to forestall the maltreatment of force, they can likewise make obstacles to definitive activity, especially when the parts of government are constrained by various ideological groups or groups with contending plans.

The impact of cash in legislative issues is another basic element that adds to the present status of political stop. Crusade funding, campaigning, and the force of particular vested parties can contort the vote based process, intensifying the voices of those with monetary assets and muffling the worries of conventional residents. The impact of cash shapes strategy needs as well as adds to a view of debasement and an absence of responsiveness in political establishments.

The electing framework itself can be a wellspring of gridlock. First-past-the-post frameworks, normal in numerous popular governments, can prompt the champ brings home all the glory results where a slight greater part in a body electorate gets all portrayal, leaving huge bits of the populace without a voice. This the champ brings home all the glory dynamic can add to a feeling of disappointment among electors whose perspectives are not reflected in the chosen delegates, further extending cultural divisions.

Verifiable heritages and social factors likewise assume a part in molding the present status of political stop. In nations with a background marked by firmly established cultural divisions, for example, ethnic or strict struggles, the scars of the past can create a long shaded area over contemporary governmental issues. These verifiable complaints can be taken advantage of by political entertainers to prepare support along personality lines, making it challenging to fashion a durable public plan that rises above authentic hatreds.

Monetary abberations and social disparities add to the feeling of political gridlock by compounding divisions inside society. At the point when certain fragments of the populace feel abandoned or minimized, there is an inclination to look for revolutionary arrangements or backing outrageous political philosophies. Tending to monetary and social incongruities isn't just an issue of civil rights yet in addition a critical part of breaking the pattern of gridlock by encouraging a more comprehensive and impartial society.

The disintegration of confidence in political organizations is both an outcome and a contributing variable to the present status of political stop. Outrages, defilement, and saw inadequacy dissolve public trust in chosen delegates and government bodies. The subsequent absence of trust makes it challenging for political pioneers to accumulate support for striking drives, and residents might become separated from the vote based process through and through.

Globalization and the interconnectedness of economies have acquainted new difficulties that contribute with the present status of political gridlock. Issues like exchange arrangements, peaceful accords, and reactions to worldwide difficulties like environmental change require composed endeavors across borders. In any case, patriot opinions and an emphasis on homegrown needs can thwart global participation, prompting strategic stalemates and obstructing the capacity to successfully address shared difficulties.

The job of political authority is essential in forming the present status of political halt. The style of authority, the obligation to discourse and think twice about, the capacity to explore different sentiments all impact the political environment. In circumstances where pioneers focus on sectarian interests over the benefit of all or participate in fierce legislative issues, the probability of gridlock increments.

The job of vested parties and campaigning in forming political plans can't be ignored. Strong vested parties, addressing corporate interests, support associations, or explicit ventures, employ critical impact in molding strategy needs. The monetary help given by these gatherings to political missions can make conditions that impact direction, further adding to the ensnarement of political gridlock.

Social and social movements, remembering changes for socioeconomics and generational mentalities, additionally impact the present status of political stop. As social orders advance, so too do the qualities and needs of their residents. The conflict among conventional and moderate qualities, generational partitions, and advancing social standards can make pressure inside political frameworks, making it trying to track down agreement on petulant issues.

The effect of the present status of political gridlock is extensive and contacts each part of society. One of the most prompt outcomes is the loss of motion of authoritative bodies, prompting the powerlessness to pass fundamental regulation. Issues, for example, foundation improvement, medical care change, and reactions to emergencies like the Coronavirus pandemic might be obstructed, leaving social orders unprepared to address squeezing difficulties.

Monetary results are additionally huge. Vulnerability emerging from political gridlock can hose financial backer certainty, obstruct monetary development, and hinder the execution of financial arrangements. The failure to address long haul monetary difficulties, for example, pay imbalance and labor force uprooting because of mechanical headways, can worsen social and financial variations inside society.

The disintegration of confidence in political organizations has significant ramifications for the working of majority rule governments. At the point when residents lose confidence in the adequacy of popularity based processes, the gamble of political unresponsiveness and separation rises. The disintegration of vote based standards and the ascent of libertarian developments or tyrant propensities might turn out to be more probable as dissatisfaction with conventional political designs develops.

Social divisions and polarization are exacerbated by the present status of political stop. Issues like migration, personality legislative issues, and civil rights become milestones where compromise appears to be slippery. The subsequent cultural disunity can appear in fights, social developments, and a breakdown in city union as residents wrestle with disparate dreams for what's in store.

On the global stage, the present status of political stop hampers the capacity of countries to really team up. Political pressures, exchange questions, and an absence of agreement on worldwide difficulties hinder progress on issues that request composed global endeavors. The outcomes are felt in the lacking reaction to transnational issues, for example, environmental change, movement, and general wellbeing emergencies.

Breaking liberated from the present status of political halt requires a comprehensive and key methodology. Tending to the main drivers includes changes at different levels, enveloping political establishments, appointive frameworks, crusade funding, and social and monetary strategies. Cultivating a culture of coordinated effort, exchange, and compromise is similarly imperative for exploring the intricacies of contemporary administration.

As far as institutional changes, an assessment of the balanced governance inside administration structures is fundamental. Finding some kind of harmony between forestalling the maltreatment of force and working with unequivocal activity is a fragile errand that requires a nuanced approach. Changes might incorporate returning to electing frameworks to guarantee more noteworthy portrayal, tending to crusade finance guidelines, and assessing the adequacy of systems intended to encourage collaboration among various parts of government.

Straightforwardness and responsibility should be focused on to revamp trust in political organizations. Open correspondence, availability of data, and measures to consider chose authorities responsible for their activities are basic parts of reestablishing confidence in the majority rule process. Incorporating straightforwardness into dynamic cycles can demystify administration and make a feeling of divided liability between residents.

Monetary and social changes are necessary to addressing the basic differences that add to the present status of political gridlock. Arrangements that focus on comprehensive financial development, evenhanded circulation of assets, and admittance to open doors can alleviate divisions inside society. Civil rights drives, instructive changes, and designated intercessions can inspire underestimated networks and make a more evenhanded starting point for administration.

Transforming the electing system is a critical part of breaking the pattern of political gridlock. Investigating elective democratic frameworks, like positioned decision casting a ballot or corresponding portrayal, can offer more nuanced impressions of different sentiments inside society. Crusade finance change and endeavors to lessen the impact of particular vested parties can relieve the effect of cash in legislative issues, cultivating a more level battleground.

Advancing a culture of cooperation and compromise is fundamental for beating the present status of political halt. Political pioneers, specifically, bear the obligation of establishing a vibe that values collaboration over conflict. Embracing the soul of bipartisanship and cultivating a pledge to figuring out some mutual interest on issues of public importance are significant for breaking the pattern of settled in political divisions.

Worldwide participation is basic for tending to worldwide difficulties that rise above public boundaries. Strategy, cooperation, and a common feeling of obligation are indispensable for exploring issues, for example, environmental change, pandemics, and financial emergencies. Fortifying global establishments and encouraging a feeling of solidarity despite shared difficulties can relieve the effect of gridlock on the world stage.

The present status of political gridlock is a mind boggling and interconnected snare of elements that request cautious assessment and key arrangements. Following the strings of gridlock through the domains of political belief system, media polarization, institutional plan, monetary inconsistencies, and social movements gives a complete comprehension of the difficulties within reach. Breaking liberated from the trap of political halt requires a promise to versatile administration, straightforwardness, responsibility, and a reestablished accentuation on the standards of a majority rules system. As social orders wrestle with the intricacies of the 21st 100 years, the basic is to explore the unpredictable elements that add to gridlock and encourage a future where coordinated effort and compromise beat division and stalemate.

Chapter 2

The Human Toll

The Human Cost of Political Stop: Disentangling the Effect on Lives and Social orders

Political stop, set apart by the powerlessness of states to arrive at agreement and establish significant strategies, claims a significant cost for living souls and social orders at large. Past the complexities of regulative gridlock and discretionary deadlocks lie unmistakable results that resonate through networks, economies, and individual prosperity. To get a handle on the full extent of the human cost, one should dive into the bunch manners by which political stalemate shapes the lived encounters of residents and makes a permanent imprint on the texture of social orders.

One of the most prompt and unmistakable appearances of political gridlock is the effect on open administrations and foundation. At the point when regulative bodies are incapacitated by gridlock, the section of financial plans and urgent regulation is frequently deferred or impeded. This, thus, upsets the financing and execution of crucial administrations like medical care, schooling, and public security. Clinics might battle with deficient assets, schools might need fundamental financing for projects, and fundamental administrations might be shortened, leaving residents helpless against a decrease in the personal satisfaction.

Medical services, specifically, endures the worst part of political stop as states wrestle with financing portions and strategy choices. The absence of agreement on medical services change can frustrate the execution of thorough and open medical services frameworks. Residents might confront boundaries to fundamental clinical benefits, experience defers in medicines, or end up troubled by the monetary kind of medical services costs. The human cost is obvious in expanded dismalness and death rates, as people wrestle with the outcomes of deficient medical care arrangement.

The instructive scene is comparatively impacted by political stop, with suggestions for people in the future. Postpones in passing training spending plans and changes can result in underfunded schools, obsolete educational programs, and lacking assets for educators and understudies. The human cost is borne by understudies who face sub-standard learning conditions, instructors who battle with restricted help, and the more extensive society that fights with the drawn out effect of a uninformed people on monetary efficiency and social attachment.

Financial results pose a potential threat in the shadow of political stop, influencing people and networks the same. At the point when legislatures neglect to pass spending plans or carry out monetary changes, vulnerability wins in monetary business sectors, hampering venture and financial development. Joblessness rates might increase, and open positions might decrease as organizations wonder whether or not to grow in that frame of mind of political precariousness. The human cost is unmistakably obvious in the existences of the people who lose their positions, wrestle with monetary frailty, and face the drawn out results of financial slumps on private prosperity.

Social government assistance programs, intended to give a security net to weak populaces, frequently become losses from political gridlock. Conflicts over subsidizing and the extent of social projects can bring about slices to help for the jobless, the old, and those confronting financial difficulty. The human cost is borne by people and families who wind up without fundamental help, confronting expanded difficulties in addressing essential requirements like lodging, food, and medical services.

The results of political stop are not restricted to the homegrown circle; they reach out to the worldwide stage, influencing global participation and reactions to shared difficulties. Issues, for example, environmental change, pandemics, and international struggles request composed endeavors with respect to countries. At the point when political gridlock blocks strategic drives and discourages coordinated effort, the human cost is apparent in the deficiency of worldwide reactions to emergencies that rise above borders.

Migration strategies are many times snared in political gridlock, influencing the existences of people looking for shelter or a superior life in another country.

Conflicts over movement change can prompt the stagnation of strategies that address the requirements of displaced people and travelers. The human cost is unmistakable in the tales of uprooted people who face dubious fates, frequently trapped in the crossfire of political discussions that decide their admittance to somewhere safe and opportunity.

One of the more guileful parts of the human cost of political stop is the disintegration of confidence in just establishments. At the point when residents witness their chosen delegates participated in unending gridlock, the confidence in the majority rule process reduces. This disintegration of trust can prompt separation from community life, as people feel that their voices are unheard and their votes ineffective. The human cost is clear in the dissatisfaction of residents who might pull out from dynamic support, adding to a debilitating of the popularity based texture.

The mental effect of political gridlock ought to be acknowledged with a sober mind. The ceaseless condition of vulnerability and the apparent absence of organization in molding one's future can add to pressure, uneasiness, and a feeling of feebleness among residents. The human cost is reflected in the psychological wellness challenges looked by people exploring the vulnerabilities made by political stalemate, as the steady condition of motion negatively affects their profound prosperity.

Social union, a foundation of steady and flourishing social orders, is risked by political stop. At the point when polarization strengthens, and political groups dig in themselves in resistance, the texture of social solidarity starts to shred. The human cost is apparent in the extending divisions inside networks, the breakdown of common talk, and the rise of social contentions filled by political enmities.

The effect of political halt on minimized and weak populaces is frequently unbalanced. Civil rights drives and strategies intended to address fundamental imbalances might be frustrated by gridlock, propagating patterns of separation and burden. The human cost is apparent in the exacerbated differences looked by minimized networks, as they wrestle with the outcomes of inaction on issues like racial shamefulness, orientation disparity, and financial imbalance.

The disintegration of conciliatory drives and worldwide collaboration because of political stop enjoys extreme ramifications for worldwide harmony and security. International pressures, arms races, and the powerlessness to fashion bound together reactions to clashes make a reality where the ghost of war poses a potential threat. The human cost is borne by those straightforwardly impacted by furnished clashes, uprooted from their homes and networks, confronting viciousness and weakness as strategic endeavors vacillate.

Natural approaches, critical for tending to the existential danger of environmental change, frequently face obstacle notwithstanding political gridlock. Conflicts over the direness of ecological activity, combined with protection from administrative measures, frustrate the capacity to execute extensive procedures. The human cost is obviously apparent in the networks that endure the worst part of ecological debasement, cataclysmic events, and the drawn out results of environmental change.

The effect of political halt on the legal executive is one more feature of the human cost. At the point when political polarization reaches out to the arrangement of judges or the affirmation of legal candidates, the freedom and viability of the legal executive might be compromised. The human cost is felt by people looking for equity, as legitimate cycles become snared in political contemplations, prompting postponements and vulnerabilities in the goal of lawful questions.

Media polarization, filled by the troublesome idea of political halt, adds to the spread of falsehood and the disintegration of genuine reporting. The human cost is clear in the disintegration of public talk, as residents are presented to one-sided stories that build up previous convictions. The subsequent protected, closed off areas thwart the capacity to take part in educated and valuable discourse, further extending cultural divisions.

The disintegration of discretionary drives and worldwide participation because of political stop finds serious ramifications for worldwide harmony and security. International pressures, arms races, and the failure to manufacture brought together reactions to clashes make a reality where the ghost of war poses a potential threat. The human cost is borne by those straightforwardly impacted by equipped contentions, uprooted from their homes and networks, confronting viciousness and uncertainty as political endeavors vacillate.

Tending to the human cost of political halt requires a complete and multi-pronged methodology. Changes at the institutional level, including changes to electing frameworks and mission finance guidelines, can moderate the effect of cash in legislative issues and encourage a more delegate and responsive government. Reinforcing social security nets, focusing on civil rights drives, and tending to foundational imbalances are fundamental parts of breaking the pattern of human experiencing sustained by political stalemate.

Developing a culture of discourse, split the difference, and joint effort is basic for conquering the human cost of political stop. Political pioneers, specifically, bear the obligation of establishing a vibe that values participation over conflict. Cultivating a pledge to figuring out some shared interest on issues of public and worldwide importance is significant for breaking the pattern of dug in political divisions.

Worldwide collaboration and tact assume a vital part in relieving the human cost of political gridlock on the worldwide stage. Political endeavors to determine clashes, address shared difficulties, and cultivate joint effort should rise above international contentions and focus on the prosperity of mankind. Reinforcing worldwide organizations and systems for coordination is fundamental for exploring the complicated trap of worldwide issues.

Putting resources into emotional wellness assets and emotionally supportive networks is pivotal for tending to the mental effect of political halt on people and networks. Perceiving the significance of mental prosperity as a general wellbeing need is indispensable to building versatile social orders that can endure the difficulties presented by political stalemate.

Advancing media education and supporting objective news coverage are fundamental parts of alleviating the human cost of political gridlock. Teaching residents on knowing tenable data, cultivating decisive reasoning abilities, and supporting free news sources are pivotal for making a very much educated public that can participate in valuable exchange.

The human cost of political halt is a profoundly instilled part of contemporary administration that requests critical consideration and purposeful endeavors to break liberated from the traps that propagate languishing. From the disintegration of public administrations to the cracking of social attachment and the worsening of worldwide difficulties, the outcomes are extensive and influence the existences of people and networks across the globe. Addressing the human cost requires a pledge to versatile administration, straightforwardness, responsibility, and a reestablished accentuation on the standards of a majority rules government and the prosperity, everything being equal. As social orders defy the difficulties of the 21st 100 years, the basic is to unwind the complicated trap of political halt and weave another account that focuses on cooperation, sympathy, and the common mankind that ties all of us.

2.1 Exploration of the various ways in which political stalemate affects the lives of ordinary people.

Investigation of the Human Effect: How Political Impasse Reverberates in the Existences of Customary Individuals

Political impasse, portrayed by a persevering absence of understanding and participation among political entertainers, creates an expansive shaded area that broadens well past the passages of force. The effect on the existences of customary individuals is diverse, addressing different parts of their reality, from admittance to fundamental administrations to the general prosperity of networks. To unwind the complicated snare of outcomes, one should investigate the different manners by which political impasse resounds through the texture of social orders, affecting the everyday encounters of people and molding their way of living.

One of the prompt and substantial outcomes of political impasse is the blocked advancement in policymaking and regulative drives. While contradicting political groups are halted in disagreements about main points of contention, the section of urgent regulation might be postponed or out and out foiled. This gridlock upsets the execution of approaches that straightforwardly influence the existences of conventional individuals, from medical services and training to social government assistance programs. Thus, residents might end up trapped in a never-ending condition of vulnerability, with the advantages of very much created strategies evading them.

Medical services, as a basic part of individual prosperity, is especially powerless with the impacts of political impasse. Stagnation in medical services change and the failure to arrive at agreement on fundamental issues can impede the execution of complete and available medical care frameworks. The outcomes are borne by standard individuals who might confront hindrances to fundamental clinical benefits, experience postpones in medicines, or wrestle with the monetary type of medical services costs. The human cost is obvious in expanded grimness rates and decreased in general wellbeing results.

The field of training is comparatively impacted, as political impasse upsets the section of schooling spending plans and thorough changes. At the point when political groups can't figure out some mutual interest on financing designations or instructive strategies, schools might confront underfunding, obsolete educational plans, and an absence of assets for instructors and understudies. The human cost is felt by understudies who experience poor learning conditions, instructors who battle with restricted help, and society at large, which fights with the drawn out results of a uninformed people on monetary efficiency and social union.

Financial outcomes echo through networks when political impasse discourages the section of spending plans and monetary changes. Vulnerability in monetary business sectors, hampered venture, and financial stagnation can bring about increasing joblessness rates and a shortage of open positions. Conventional individuals might wind up wrestling with monetary instability, employment misfortunes, and the drawn out effect of financial slumps on private prosperity. The monetary cost of political impasse stretches out past individual lives, influencing the general thriving of networks and social orders.

Social government assistance programs, intended to give a security net to weak populaces, frequently become losses from political impasse. Conflicts over subsidizing and the extent of social projects can prompt cuts in help for the jobless, the older, and those confronting monetary difficulty. The human cost is obvious in the battles of people and families who end up without fundamental help, confronting expanded difficulties in addressing essential requirements like lodging, food, and medical services.

The results of political impasse are not restricted to the homegrown circle; they reach out to the worldwide stage, influencing global participation and reactions to shared difficulties. Issues, for example, environmental change, pandemics, and international struggles request composed endeavors with respect to countries. At the point when political stop hinders strategic drives and deters coordinated effort, the human cost is obvious in the deficiency of worldwide reactions to emergencies that rise above borders.

Movement strategies, ensnared in political gridlock, influence the existences of people looking for shelter or a superior life in another country. Conflicts over migration change can prompt strategy stagnation, leaving people in a condition of vulnerability. The human cost is unmistakable in the accounts of dislodged people who face dubious fates, frequently trapped in the crossfire of political discussions that decide their admittance to somewhere safe and opportunity.

The disintegration of confidence in equitable establishments is an unpretentious yet unavoidable outcome of political impasse. At the point when residents witness their chosen agents participated in ceaseless gridlock, the confidence in the majority rule process reduces. This disintegration of trust can prompt withdrawal from urban life, as people feel that their voices are unheard and their votes inadequate. The human cost is obvious in the bafflement of residents who might pull out from dynamic cooperation, adding to a debilitating of the majority rule texture.

The mental effect of political impasse ought to be considered carefully. The ceaseless condition of vulnerability and the apparent absence of organization in molding one's future can add to pressure, tension, and a feeling of frailty among residents. The human cost is reflected in the emotional wellness challenges looked by people exploring the vulnerabilities made by political stalemate, as the consistent condition of transition negatively affects their close to home prosperity.

Social union, a foundation of steady and flourishing social orders, is imperiled by political impasse. At the point when polarization escalates, and political groups dig in themselves in resistance, the texture of social solidarity starts to shred. The human cost is noticeable in the extending divisions inside networks, the breakdown of common talk, and the rise of social contentions filled by political hostilities.

The effect of political impasse on minimized and weak populaces is frequently unbalanced. Civil rights drives and approaches intended to address fundamental disparities might be frustrated by gridlock, sustaining patterns of segregation and detriment. The human cost is obvious in the exacerbated variations looked by underestimated networks, as they wrestle with the outcomes of inaction on issues like racial foul play, orientation imbalance, and financial disparity.

The disintegration of discretionary drives and worldwide collaboration because of political impasse experiences serious ramifications for worldwide harmony and security. International strains, arms races, and the failure to manufacture brought together reactions to clashes make a reality where the ghost of war poses a potential threat. The human cost is borne by those straightforwardly impacted by outfitted clashes, uprooted from their homes and networks, confronting savagery and frailty as discretionary endeavors flounder.

Ecological arrangements, vital for tending to the existential danger of environmental change, frequently face block notwithstanding political impasse. Conflicts over the direness of natural activity, combined with protection from administrative measures, thwart the capacity to execute complete systems. The human cost is obviously clear in the networks that endure the worst part of ecological debasement, catastrophic events, and the drawn out results of environmental change.

The effect of political impasse on the legal executive is one more aspect of the human cost. At the point when political polarization stretches out to the arrangement of judges or the affirmation of legal chosen people, the freedom and adequacy of the legal executive might be compromised. The human cost is felt by people looking for equity, as legitimate cycles become entrapped in political contemplations, prompting deferrals and vulnerabilities in the goal of lawful debates.

Media polarization, filled by the disruptive idea of political impasse, adds to the spread of deception and the disintegration of genuine news-casting. The human cost is clear in the disintegration of public talk, as residents are presented to one-sided stories that support previous convictions. The subsequent protected, closed off areas ruin the capacity to participate in educated and valuable discourse, further extending cultural divisions.

Tending to the human cost of political impasse requires a complete and multi-pronged methodology. Changes at the institutional level, including changes to discretionary frameworks and mission finance guidelines, can relieve the effect of cash in legislative issues and cultivate a more delegate and responsive government.

Reinforcing social security nets, focusing on civil rights drives, and tending to foundational imbalances are fundamental parts of breaking the pattern of human experiencing propagated by political stalemate.

Developing a culture of discourse, split the difference, and joint effort is basic for defeating the human cost of political impasse. Political pioneers, specifically, bear the obligation of establishing a vibe that values collaboration over conflict. Encouraging a pledge to settling on some shared interest on issues of public and worldwide importance is essential for breaking the pattern of dug in political divisions.

Worldwide participation and tact assume a urgent part in moderating the human cost of political impasse on the worldwide stage. Strategic endeavors to determine clashes, address shared difficulties, and encourage cooperation should rise above international contentions and focus on the prosperity of mankind. Reinforcing worldwide foundations and components for coordination is fundamental for exploring the intricate trap of worldwide issues.

Putting resources into emotional wellness assets and emotionally supportive networks is urgent for tending to the mental effect of political impasse on people and networks. Perceiving the significance of mental prosperity as a general wellbeing need is vital to building strong social orders that can endure the difficulties presented by political stalemate.

Advancing media proficiency and supporting objective news coverage are fundamental parts of relieving the human cost of political impasse. Teaching residents on knowing dependable data, encouraging decisive reasoning abilities, and supporting free news sources are essential for making a very much educated public that can take part in productive exchange.

The investigation of the different manners by which political impasse influences the existences of common individuals uncovers a mind boggling exchange of outcomes that shape the day to day encounters of people and networks. From the disintegration of fundamental administrations to the breaking of social union and the intensification of worldwide difficulties, the effect is sweeping and requests consideration. Addressing the human cost requires a promise to versatile administration, straightforwardness, responsibility, and a recharged accentuation on the standards of a majority rules government and the prosperity, everything being equal. As social orders explore the difficulties of the 21st hundred years, the basic is to unwind the perplexing snare of political impasse and weave another story that focuses on cooperation, empathy, and the common humankind that ties every one of us.

2.2 Highlighting specific instances of human suffering linked to political inaction.

Occurrences of Human Experiencing Connected to Political Inaction: A Call to Address the Outcomes

Political inaction, frequently coming about because of impasses and gridlock, has substantial and annihilating outcomes on the existences of people and networks.

The human experiencing connected to political idleness appears across different areas, from medical care and schooling to financial abberations and natural difficulties. To genuinely comprehend the profundity of these results, one should investigate explicit occasions where political inaction has exacerbated human misery, leaving a path of difficulty that stretches out a long ways past the corridors of government.

In the domain of medical care, occasions of human enduring are obviously apparent when political inaction impedes the execution of far reaching medical care changes. The shortfall of a brought together obligation to open and quality medical care departs residents helpless against a bunch of difficulties. One glaring model is the absence of general medical services in numerous countries, where the shortfall of a strong strategy system brings about people confronting extravagant clinical expenses, restricted admittance to fundamental therapies, and, at times, being compelled to renounce vital clinical consideration because of monetary imperatives.

The US, notwithstanding being perhaps of the richest country, fills in as an impactful outline of this peculiarity. The shortfall of a vigorous, generally open medical care framework has left millions without satisfactory inclusion, prompting deferred or predestined clinical therapies, preventable wellbeing emergencies, and a huge weight of clinical obligation. Political inaction on medical care change propagates a framework where the nature of clinical consideration is much of not entirely set in stone by financial status, worsening existing wellbeing differences and causing boundless languishing over those unfit to manage the cost of fundamental therapies.

Essentially, with regards to general wellbeing emergencies, the results of political inaction become extremely obvious. The worldwide reaction to the Coronavirus pandemic highlights the effect of postponed and lacking measures. Occurrences where state run administrations neglect to carry out opportune and facilitated reactions lead to overpowered medical services frameworks, high death rates, and delayed times of financial and social disturbance.

Nations that accomplished political gridlock and postponed decision-production during the underlying phases of the pandemic confronted serious results. Deficient testing, an absence of individual defensive hardware, and postponed immunization crusades added to the spread of the infection and expanded human misery. The cost of lost lives, stressed medical care experts, and the financial difficulties persevered by people and organizations fills in as an unmistakable sign of the significant ramifications of political inaction even with a general wellbeing emergency.

Schooling, as a key right and key determinant of individual and cultural prosperity, is another space where political inaction claims a cost for human torment. Occasions where policymakers neglect to focus on training, institute vital changes, or dispense adequate assets lead to a scope of unfortunate results. In many examples, underestimated networks endure the worst part of instructive variations, propagating patterns of destitution and disparity.

In locales where political inaction obstructs the execution of complete training changes, schools frequently need satisfactory subsidizing, qualified educators, and fundamental assets. Understudies from distraught foundations face obstructions to learning, with restricted admittance to innovation, extracurricular exercises, and high level coursework. The outcome is an instructive separation that compounds existing social disparities, restricting open doors for up versatility and sustaining patterns of destitution.

Struggle zones give impactful instances of how political inaction can prompt the boundless enduring of kids denied of instruction. In locales tormented by outfitted struggle, for example, portions of Africa and the Center East, the disturbance of school systems because of political dormancy passes on ages of kids without admittance to tutoring. The outcomes are significant, as absence of instruction hampers individual improvement as well as blocks the possibilities of post-struggle recuperation and the remaking of stable social orders.

Financial inconsistencies, exacerbated by political inaction, contribute essentially to human affliction, broadening the hole between the special and the underestimated. In occasions where legislatures neglect to resolve fundamental issues, for example, pay disparity, absence of social wellbeing nets, and biased financial approaches, the results are desperate for weak populaces. The augmenting abundance hole prompts expanded neediness, restricted admittance to fundamental administrations, and limited open doors for financial headway.

One of the most over the top glaring instances of financial experiencing connected to political inaction is the steadiness of outrageous neediness in many areas of the planet. In areas where states disregard to carry out far reaching destitution easing techniques, people and networks persevere through the difficulties of lacking admittance to food, clean water, schooling, and medical services. The propagation of neediness turns into a cycle that rises above ages, denying people of the opportunity to break liberated from the shackles of dejection.

In the fallout of monetary emergencies, political inaction can fuel the enduring of weak populaces. The 2008 worldwide monetary emergency is a piercing model where the absence of quick and composed activity by legislatures prompted far reaching joblessness, home dispossessions, and financial difficulties for millions. People confronted employment misfortunes, decreasing reserve funds, and, much of the time, the deficiency of homes and livelihoods. The outcomes of political inaction during financial slumps reverberation for quite a long time, adding to a feeling of dissatisfaction and dissolving trust in legislative organizations.

Social government assistance programs, intended to give a wellbeing net to weak populaces, frequently succumb to political inaction. Cases where legislatures neglect to address the deficiencies of social wellbeing nets bring about expanded human affliction, especially for those confronting financial difficulty, joblessness, or wellbeing challenges. The disintegration of social government assistance programs fuels the weakness of underestimated populaces, leaving them without fundamental help during critical crossroads.

In nations with deficient social wellbeing nets, for example, portions of sub-Saharan Africa, people and families are left without a dependable method for help during emergencies. The results are especially desperate during occasions like catastrophic events, where the absence of social help increases the enduring of the individuals who lose their homes, vocations, and friends and family. Political inaction in reinforcing social wellbeing nets sustains patterns of destitution and passes on weak populaces without the essential assets to modify their lives.

Political inaction likewise assumes a critical part in compounding the enduring of dislodged populaces, including evacuees and inside uprooted people. Occasions where state run administrations neglect to address the underlying drivers of relocation, give satisfactory compassionate help, or carry out complete resettlement programs add to the delayed enduring of those compelled to escape their homes.

The predicament of Syrian exiles fills in as a powerful illustration of the results of political inaction in tending to removal. The extended Syrian clash has prompted one of the biggest outcast emergencies in late history. Political divisions among countries, combined with an absence of deliberate endeavors to address the underlying drivers of the contention, have left huge number of Syrians in unstable circumstances. The enduring of dislodged people, living in packed exile camps with restricted admittance to essential necessities, highlights the human expense of political inaction notwithstanding philanthropic emergencies.

Ecological difficulties, including environmental change and cataclysmic events, are regions where political inaction has broad ramifications for human misery. The outcomes of deferred or deficient reactions to ecological emergencies incorporate relocation, loss of livelihoods, and expanded weakness to outrageous climate occasions.

Low-lying waterfront locales, like Bangladesh, are especially helpless to the effects of environmental change, including rising ocean levels and more incessant and serious twisters. Political inaction in carrying out alleviation and variation procedures leaves weak populaces helpless before natural changes. The enduring of people who lose their homes, livelihoods, and friends and family because of environment incited debacles is an unmistakable indication of the human cost when legislatures neglect to make a definitive move to address natural difficulties.

The effect of political inaction on the legal framework adds to human enduring by blocking admittance to equity and propagating treacheries. Cases where political polarization slows down the arrangement of judges or impedes legal cycles bring about deferred legal procedures and an absence of responsibility for bad behavior.

Nations where political impedance in the legal framework is common frequently witness denials of basic liberties, defilement, and an absence of change for casualties. The enduring of people who are denied equity is significant, as they wrestle with the results of uncontrolled power, exemption, and the disintegration of law and order. The shortfall of a fair and successful legal framework propagates a pattern of human torment, leaving casualties without response and cultivating a culture of exemption.

Media polarization, filled by political inaction, adds to the spread of falsehood and the disintegration of true reporting. The outcomes of a spellbound media scene incorporate the twisting of realities, the control of popular assessment, and the sabotaging of vote based values.

Occurrences where political pioneers sustain deception or take part in assaults on the media add to an environment where truth is clouded, and public talk is harmed. The enduring is obvious in the disintegration of confidence in data sources, the polarization of social orders, and the difficulties looked by residents attempting to explore a complex and quickly impacting world. The outcomes of media polarization reach out past individual lives, molding the actual texture of majority rule social orders.

Addressing the occurrences of human experiencing connected to political inaction requires a multi-layered and proactive methodology. Changes at the institutional level, including changes to constituent frameworks, crusade finance guidelines, and the fortifying of governing rules, can moderate the effect of cash in legislative issues and encourage a more delegate and responsive government.

Putting resources into social wellbeing nets and exhaustive destitution lightening methodologies is critical for moderating the enduring of weak populaces. State run administrations should focus on the prosperity of their residents by guaranteeing admittance to fundamental administrations, schooling, medical services, and monetary open doors. Worldwide collaboration is basic, especially in tending to worldwide difficulties, for example, pandemics, environmental change, and philanthropic emergencies.

Encouraging a culture of exchange, split the difference, and cooperation is fundamental for beating the human experiencing connected to political inaction. Political pioneers, specifically, bear the obligation of establishing a vibe that values participation over conflict. Embracing the soul of bipartisanship and encouraging a pledge to figuring out some shared interest on issues of public and worldwide importance are urgent for breaking the pattern of settled in political divisions.

The particular examples of human experiencing connected to political inaction feature the significant results that stretch out from the passageways of capacity to the regular routines of people and networks. Whether in medical care, training, financial differences, or natural difficulties, the cost of political latency is obvious in the tales of the people who persevere through pointless difficulties. Tending to these examples requires underlying changes as well as an aggregate obligation to the standards of equity, value, and the prosperity, everything being equal. As social orders face the difficulties of the 21st hundred years, the basic is to gain from these occasions, break liberated from the shackles of political inaction, and manufacture a way toward a future where human enduring is reduced through proactive and sympathetic administration.

2.3 Analysis of the social, economic, and health consequences of prolonged political gridlock.

Examination of the Social, Monetary, and Wellbeing Results of Delayed Political Gridlock

Drawn out political gridlock, described by a determined absence of understanding and participation among political entertainers, has expansive results that pervade the texture of social orders. The effect ranges across friendly, financial, and wellbeing areas, molding the lived encounters of people and networks. In this examination, we dig into the mind boggling elements that unfurl when political frameworks come to a standstill, investigating the diverse outcomes that unfurl after some time.

Social Outcomes: Broke People group and Dissolved Trust

One of the most discernible social outcomes of delayed political gridlock is the breaking of networks and the disintegration of confidence in just foundations. At the point when political groups stay halted, incapable to settle on some shared interest on central questions, cultural divisions extend, and common talk gives way to polarization. This polarization is frequently exacerbated by media accounts that enhance hardliner perspectives, making protected, closed off environments that build up existing convictions.

As people group become captivated, the feeling of a common public personality debilitates. Trust in administrative foundations declines, and residents might feel disengaged from the political cycle. The disintegration of social union is especially clear in the breakdown of common talk, as people progressively view those with contrasting political convictions as enemies as opposed to kinsmen. This fracture of social bonds adds to a feeling of distance and lessens the feeling of aggregate liability regarding the prosperity of society.

Monetary Outcomes: Stagnation and Vulnerability

Delayed political gridlock claims a weighty cost for monetary solidness and development. The powerlessness to pass financial plans, execute monetary changes, and settle on convenient choices establishes a climate of vulnerability that hampers venture and monetary turn of events. Organizations, dubious about the future administrative and financial scene, may defer development plans or cut back on speculations, prompting stagnation and an absence of occupation creation.

The 2013 U.S. government closure fills in as a clear illustration of the financial results of political gridlock. The closure, coming about because of an inability to pass a bureaucratic spending plan, prompted leaves of administrative specialists, postponed taxpayer driven organizations, and a decrease in purchaser and business certainty. The gradually expanding influences were felt all through the economy, with gauges demonstrating a decrease in financial development and occupation creation.

Additionally, drawn out political gridlock can impede the section of thorough financial changes. Issues like expense strategies, foundation ventures, and economic accords might stay unsettled, forestalling the execution of measures significant for cultivating monetary strength and seriousness. The monetary results stretch out past public boundaries, influencing worldwide business sectors and adding to an environment of vulnerability in the global financial scene.

Wellbeing Results: Hindrances to Public Prosperity

The effect of drawn out political gridlock on general wellbeing is significant, with suggestions for admittance to medical care, the administration of general wellbeing emergencies, and the general prosperity of networks. In circumstances where political entertainers are stopped over medical care strategies, the entry of significant changes might be deferred or impeded, leaving medical services frameworks stressed and people without fundamental administrations.

The Reasonable Consideration Act (ACA) in the US fills in as an outline of the wellbeing results of political gridlock. The disagreeable discussions and lawful difficulties encompassing the ACA prompted vulnerabilities about the eventual fate of the medical services framework. States confronted difficulties in growing Medicaid, and people were left in an in-between state with respect to admittance to reasonable health care coverage. Drawn out gridlock in tending to medical care issues can bring about an absence of admittance to preventive administrations, postponed therapies, and generally speaking lacks in the medical services framework.

Moreover, the administration of general wellbeing emergencies, like pandemics, can be seriously undermined by political gridlock. The Coronavirus pandemic featured the significance of quick and facilitated administrative reactions. Nonetheless, in occurrences where political divisions frustrate definitive activity, the results can be critical. Deferred testing, lacking assignment of assets, and conflicting general wellbeing informing add to the spread of the infection and increment the general cost for general wellbeing.

Interconnected Elements: The Endless loop of Gridlock

These social, monetary, and wellbeing results are not separated; they structure an interconnected web that propagates an endless loop of gridlock. For example, monetary stagnation coming about because of political gridlock can add to social distress as joblessness rises and pay imbalance augments. This social agitation, thusly, further enraptures networks and strains social attachment, making it much more trying for political entertainers to figure out something worth agreeing on.

Similarly, wellbeing abberations can intensify existing social disparities. In the event that political gridlock obstructs the execution of wellbeing strategies pointed toward tending to these differences, weak populaces might confront expanded wellbeing gambles and decreased admittance to fundamental administrations. The subsequent stress on general wellbeing assets further mixtures monetary difficulties, as the expense of treating preventable diseases rises.

This interconnectedness stretches out to worldwide relations, as worldwide difficulties like environmental change and irresistible sicknesses require cooperative arrangements. Drawn out political gridlock on the worldwide stage can block endeavors to address these difficulties successfully, enhancing the monetary, social, and wellbeing results on a worldwide scale.

Possible Pathways to Alleviation: Breaking the Gridlock

Tending to the outcomes of delayed political gridlock requires vital mediations and a promise to breaking the cycle. Here are likely pathways to moderation:

Institutional Changes: Carrying out changes to smooth out regulative cycles, upgrade governing rules, and diminish the impact of cash in governmental issues can make a more responsive and powerful political framework. Electing changes, like positioned decision casting a ballot, may urge possibility to interest a more extensive base, decreasing polarization.

Advancing Bipartisanship: Cultivating a culture of bipartisanship is critical for conquering gridlock. Political pioneers can establish the vibe by underlining cooperation over conflict and settling on something worth agreeing on issues of public significance. Motivators for bipartisan participation, like shared arrangement victories, can be supported.

Improving Metro Instruction: Advancing urban training is fundamental for developing an educated and drew in populace. A very much educated public is better prepared to consider lawmakers responsible and partake in the popularity based process. Instruction programs that underscore decisive reasoning and media education can add to a seriously insightful electorate.

Worldwide Coordinated effort: Perceiving the interconnectedness of worldwide difficulties, countries should focus on global cooperation. Tact, collaboration on environment activity, and composed reactions to wellbeing emergencies require a guarantee to rising above international divisions for everyone's benefit.

Public Support: Common society assumes a crucial part in considering political pioneers responsible and upholding for change. Grassroots developments, promotion associations, and drew in residents can all in all push for changes, request straightforwardness, and work to connect social partitions.

A Call for Versatile Administration

The examination of the social, monetary, and wellbeing results of delayed political gridlock uncovers a perplexing interchange of elements that significantly influence the prosperity of social orders. Breaking liberated from this gridlock requires versatile administration that answers the advancing necessities of networks, encourages cooperation, and focuses on the benefit of everyone over hardliner interests.

The way ahead includes primary changes as well as a social shift that puts a superior on discourse, split the difference, and a common obligation to the standards of a majority rules system. As countries explore the difficulties of the 21st 100 years, the basic is to gain from the outcomes of drawn out political gridlock, adjust administration designs to fulfill the needs of an influencing world, and fashion a future where social orders flourish through strong, comprehensive, and responsive political frameworks.

Chapter 3

Root Causes and Structural Issues

Main drivers and Underlying Issues: Unloading the Gridlock Puzzle

In the maze of political elements, the foundations of gridlock tunnel profound into the dirt of cultural and institutional designs. Part Three of "Ensnared Gridlock: Unwinding Political Impasse and Easing Human Affliction" leaves on an odyssey to disentangle the riddle of gridlock by taking apart its basic causes and underlying issues.

Political gridlock, at its center, is much of the time established in the dirt of sectarian polarization. The polarization of political belief systems and affiliations has arrived at remarkable levels, establishing a climate where compromise turns into a setback from the philosophical milestone. The philosophical inflexibility of political entertainers, whether driven by veritable conviction or vital situating, raises considerable hindrances to agreement building. In this captivated scene, strategy choices become milestones for philosophical matchless quality as opposed to helpful endeavors to address the requirements of a different and complex society.

Also, the primary issues inside political establishments act as the platform that either upholds viable administration or disintegrates under the heaviness of hardliner friction. Constituent frameworks, intended to address the desire of individuals, can coincidentally add to gridlock. First-past-the-post frameworks, for example, may boost a two-party framework that enhances polarization and lessens the probability of different viewpoints tracking down a spot inside the political range. Corresponding portrayal, then again, while encouraging inclusivity, may prompt divided councils that battle to shape stable alliances equipped for definitive activity.

The detachment of abilities, a major precept of popularity based administration, can likewise add to gridlock when the balanced governance intended to forestall maltreatment of force become obstructions to successful administration. The three sided division of force — chief, regulative, and legal — can decay into a framework where each branch turns into a war zone for political moving, slowing down the execution of strategies and hindering the goal of basic issues.

Notwithstanding these fundamental difficulties, the impact of cash in governmental issues further confuses the scene. The ascent of strong vested parties and the flood of corporate commitments can contort strategy needs, making it trying for chose authorities for act to the greatest advantage of the more extensive populace. The gravitational draw of mission supporting can make a reliance that subverts the responsiveness of political pioneers to the requirements of their constituents, propagating a pattern of gridlock and think twice about issues critical to human government assistance.

A frequently disregarded underlying issue adding to gridlock is the job of media in molding public talk. The cutting edge media scene, with its 24-hour patterns of media reporting and emotionalism, can encourage an environment where political posing overshadows meaningful strategy conversations. The polarization and misrepresentation of perplexing issues for mass utilization add to popular assessment that is many times partitioned along hardliner lines. Thus, this further digs in lawmakers in their positions, making compromise a politically dangerous undertaking.

The disintegration of institutional standards and customs is one more basic consider the gridlock condition. At the point when laid out standards that once worked with collaboration and compromise are disposed of or controlled for momentary political addition, the actual groundworks of successful administration are sabotaged. The disintegration of confidence in foundations, combined with a feeling of distrust toward the political cycle, further extends the gorge among residents and their delegates.

Past these foundational issues, the manipulating of discretionary locale stands apart as an intense supporter of political impasse.

The intentional control of region limits to incline toward one ideological group over one more has significant ramifications for the representativeness of chosen bodies. Manipulated regions frequently bring about a lopsided designation of seats, intensifying the impact of a specific philosophical group and reducing the possibilities for cross-party coordinated effort.

To comprehend the main drivers of gridlock, recognizing the job of personality politics is essential. At the point when political talk becomes buried in character based affiliations, whether along racial, ethnic, or social lines, the potential for participation decreases. Issues that ought to be drawn nearer with an aggregate outlook are rather seen through the limited focal point of gathering character, encouraging a climate where compromise is seen as a treachery to one's local area.

The interchange of these underlying drivers and primary issues makes a mind boggling and self-supporting framework that supports political gridlock. The trap of philosophies, institutional deficiencies, and outer impacts makes a powerful coincidence that frustrates successful administration and intensifies human torment.

Breaking liberated from this gridlock puzzler requires a multi-layered approach. Changes focusing on both the fundamental issues inside political foundations and the social and cultural variables adding to polarization are fundamental. Electing change, crusade finance change, and endeavors to encourage an additional comprehensive and mindful media climate are basic parts of a technique pointed toward destroying the primary boundaries to successful administration.

All the while, remaking trust in organizations and it is basic to support majority rule standards. Pioneers should focus on the drawn out wellbeing of the majority rule process over momentary political increases. Straightforward and responsible administration can assist with overcoming any barrier among residents and their delegates, encouraging a feeling of mutual perspective and aggregate liability.

In any case, tending to the main drivers of gridlock requires more than institutional changes. It requires a social shift — a change in the manner social orders see and draw in with governmental issues. A create some distance from lose governmental issues, where one party's benefit is viewed as another's misfortune, toward a cooperative methodology that focuses on the benefit of all is fundamental. This shift requires supporting a culture that values split the difference as a strength as opposed to a shortcoming and commends variety of thought as a foundation of powerful navigation.

In the excursion to disentangle the gridlock puzzle, it becomes apparent that the foundations of political impasse are profoundly dug in, spreading over the mind boggling nexus of philosophy, establishments, and cultural elements.

Just through an extensive comprehension of these main drivers could successful techniques at any point be contrived to unravel the gridlock and prepare for a political scene that is responsive, comprehensive, and fit for resolving the major problems that influence human prosperity. As we explore this investigation, the acknowledgment of the interconnectedness of these variables becomes vital, directing us toward all encompassing arrangements that go past simple side effect mitigation and address the basic difficulties that propagate the ensnarement of legislative issues and human torment.

3.1 In-depth examination of the underlying causes of political stalemate.

Inside and out Assessment of the Fundamental Reasons for Political Impasse

To disentangle the mind boggling embroidery of political impasse, one should leave on a nuanced investigation of the fundamental causes that render administration frameworks vulnerable to inactivity. This top to bottom assessment, framing the center of Section Three in "Caught Gridlock: Unwinding Political Impasse and Reducing Human Misery," digs into the perplexing snare of variables that merge to make a scene where compromise is slippery, and progress is ruined.

At the core of political impasse lies the inescapable issue of hardliner polarization. The difference of political philosophies and the increase of party steadfastness have arrived at phenomenal levels, establishing a climate where bipartisanship turns into an intriguing item. The philosophical gap that isolates political entertainers obstructs helpful exchange and cultivates an environment where issues are moved toward not on their benefits but rather from the perspective of party connection. As the bay augments, the limit with respect to think twice about, and the authoritative interaction changes into a field where triumphs are estimated by the loss of the restricting party as opposed to the headway of the public great.

The foundations of this polarization reach out past simple philosophical contrasts. Social and social elements contribute altogether to the extending partition. Issues like character legislative issues, social qualities, and financial variations interweave with political connection, making a mind boggling lattice where people recognize with a specific political philosophy as well as with a more extensive arrangement of convictions and values related with their gatherings. In such a climate, political talk turns into a landmark of clashing personalities, fueling polarization and obstructing the quest for shared belief.

In addition, the impact of media in molding general assessment couldn't possibly be more significant. The contemporary media scene, described by 24-hour patterns of media reporting, online entertainment protected, closed off environments, and the sensationalization of political occasions, assumes an essential part in enhancing polarization.

The quest for evaluations and online commitment frequently focuses on troublesome accounts over nuanced conversations, adding to the support of prior convictions and the making of data bubbles. Residents, immersed with captivated viewpoints, become dug in their philosophical positions, making split the difference and cooperation more trying for chose authorities.

Past the domain of thoughts and character, the primary elements of political frameworks contribute fundamentally to the propagation of gridlock. The first-past-the-post constituent framework, predominant in numerous popular governments, will in general lean toward a two-party framework. While effortlessness might be an ideals in constituent plan, this framework frequently minimizes outsiders and limits the variety of political portrayal. The predominance of a two-party dynamic, especially when combined with polarization, builds up a paired way to deal with administration, generally ruling out elective viewpoints or cooperative direction.

On the other hand, corresponding portrayal, however encouraging variety, represents its own difficulties. Multi-party frameworks coming about because of corresponding portrayal can prompt divided lawmaking bodies where alliance building turns into a need for administration. While alliance legislatures can possibly address a more extensive range of perspectives, they are likewise helpless to inward disunity, convoluting the policymaking system and adding to gridlock.

The division of abilities, an essential rule in just administration, can turn into a situation with two sides. While expected to forestall the grouping of force and shield against manhandles, the division between the chief, regulative, and legal branches can prompt a dissemination of obligation. Rather than working with balanced governance, this partition can degenerate into a framework where each branch works in separation, cultivating a climate where direction becomes bulky, and the execution of strategies is full of snags.

The impact of cash in governmental issues further enhances the difficulties presented by the underlying model of political frameworks. Crusade supporting, frequently determined by strong vested parties and corporate commitments, presents a layer of intricacy that can misshape strategy needs. Chosen authorities, dependent on monetary help for their missions, may find themselves obliged to specific interests, undermining their capacity to act to the greatest advantage of the more extensive populace. The convergence of financial power and political independent direction makes a dynamic where strategy results are impacted by those with the resources to shape the political scene.

Manipulating, the intentional control of discretionary locale limits to lean toward one ideological group over another, arises as a basic supporter of political impasse. By decisively redrawing region lines, gatherings can get electing benefits that don't precisely mirror the appropriation of public opinion. Manipulated locale frequently bring about uncompetitive races, where officeholders face negligible difficulties, and the motivator to take part in bipartisan collaboration decreases. The twisting of appointive portrayal compounds polarization and debilitates the instruments intended to consider chose authorities responsible.

Notwithstanding these primary difficulties, the disintegration of institutional standards and customs further sabotages compelling administration. Laid out standards, whether casual sets of principles or bipartisan arrangements, have generally filled in as the paste that ties political entertainers chasing after shared objectives. At the point when these standards are disposed of or controlled for transient political increases, the results resound through the political framework, disintegrating the trust between political entertainers and hindering the systems that work with split the difference and joint effort.

Besides, the ascent of personality legislative issues presents a layer of intricacy that rises above philosophical contrasts. At the point when political talk becomes interlaced with personalities in light of race, identity, religion, or other social markers, the potential for cooperation decreases. Issues that ought to be tended to through an aggregate and comprehensive focal point are rather separated through the tight crystals of gathering character, dividing the political scene and upsetting the development of wide based alliances.

The exchange of these variables makes a self-building up framework where polarization, underlying hindrances, and social elements feed into one another, propagating a condition of political gridlock. The outcomes of this trap are expansive, affecting the capacity of states to answer major problems and worsening human experiencing on various fronts.

Tending to the basic reasons for political impasse requires an extensive and multi-pronged methodology. At the primary level, discretionary changes that advance inclusivity, crusade finance changes that relieve the impact of cash in legislative issues, and redistricting changes that check manipulating are fundamental stages toward establishing a more favorable climate for viable administration.

All the while, endeavors to encourage a culture of joint effort and compromise are significant. Training and public talk drives can assume a part in advancing media education and decisive reasoning, empowering residents to explore the data scene all the more successfully. Empowering political pioneers to focus on the drawn out soundness of popularity based organizations over momentary political additions is basic for modifying trust in the political cycle.

Developing a feeling of shared character and reason, rising above disruptive markers, is fundamental for relieving the effect of personality legislative issues. Underlining the normal mankind that ties people across political and social partitions can make ready for a more comprehensive and sympathetic political talk.

The top to bottom assessment of the basic reasons for political impasse uncovers a perplexing and interconnected snare of elements. From philosophical polarization to primary difficulties inside political frameworks and the impact of cash in legislative issues, the snare of these components propagates a condition of gridlock that impedes viable administration.

Unwinding this web requires a comprehensive comprehension of the elements at play, combined with key changes and social moves that cultivate cooperation, inclusivity, and a restored obligation to the standards of a vote based system. Just through such an extensive methodology might we at any point desire to break liberated from the hold of political impasse and lighten the human experiencing that goes with it.

3.2 Discussion on structural issues within political systems that contribute to deadlock.

Conversation on Primary Issues inside Political Frameworks that Add to Gridlock

Section Three of "Trapped Gridlock: Unwinding Political Impasse and Mitigating Human Misery" embraces a complete conversation on the underlying issues inside political frameworks, analyzing the instruments that add to the obstinate issue of political halt. As we explore this conversation, it becomes obvious that the underlying foundations of gridlock are profoundly implanted in the actual underpinnings of administration structures, requiring a basic assessment of discretionary frameworks, the detachment of abilities, and the impact of cash in legislative issues.

Appointive Frameworks: Molding the Scene of Political Contest

At the core of the conversation on primary issues lies the plan of electing frameworks. These frameworks, expected to make an interpretation of resident inclinations into political portrayal, assume a significant part in forming the scene of political rivalry. In any case, their effect on halt becomes evident when we think about the repercussions of explicit plans.

The first-past-the-post (FPTP) discretionary framework, broadly embraced in majoritarian popular governments, adds to a two-party strength that can heighten polarization. FPTP grants triumph to the up-and-comer with the most votes in every body electorate, making a champ brings home all the glory dynamic. While effortlessness is many times refered to as a righteousness, the situation will in general sideline outsiders, building up a parallel way to deal with administration. In such a framework, the desires of more modest gatherings and different viewpoints battle to track down portrayal, restricting the scope of strategy choices and propagating the polarization that describes contemporary governmental issues.

On the other hand, relative portrayal (PR) frameworks expect to convey seats with respect to the general vote portion of ideological groups. While PR encourages a more different portrayal of political philosophies, it accompanies its own arrangement of difficulties. Multi-party frameworks coming about because of PR can prompt divided governing bodies where alliance building turns into a need. While alliances can hypothetically address a more extensive range of perspectives, they frequently face inside strains, going with durable choice making and strategy execution more troublesome.

The effect of constituent frameworks on gridlock stretches out past the arrangement of governing bodies. The champ brings home all the glory idea of FPTP can prompt unpredictable swings between ideological groups, establishing a climate where strategy inversions are regular. Such unpredictability adds to an absence of strategy coherence, blocking long haul arranging and encouraging a climate where each new organization looks to destroy the drives of its ancestor. This absence of progression can block the execution of compelling, supported strategies, adding to the view of administration as a progression of disconnected, momentary measures.

Resolving the primary issue of constituent frameworks requires cautious thought of the compromises among straightforwardness and portrayal. Changes pointed toward presenting components of proportionality, like blended part frameworks, or positioned decision casting a ballot, can encourage a more comprehensive political scene, where different voices track down articulation without forfeiting the security important for successful administration.

The Division of Abilities: Balanced governance or Barriers to Activity?

Vital to the idea of popularity based administration is the detachment of abilities among the leader, authoritative, and legal branches. This division is planned to forestall the convergence of force, defend against manhandles, and guarantee that each branch goes about as a keep an eye on the others. Nonetheless, when analyzed with regards to halt, the detachment of abilities can turn into a blade that cuts both ways.

While governing rules are fundamental for forestalling tyranny, an excessively inflexible detachment can impede productive independent direction. The three sided division can prompt a dissemination of obligation, making it trying to organize strategy drives across branches. The particular jobs and locales of each branch, while planned to forestall maltreatments of force, can likewise bring about a framework where navigation is divided and inclined to delays.

Besides, the arrangement of balanced governance can make a scene where political entertainers decisively send their powers to hinder drives as opposed to team up for a long term benefit. The delay in the U.S. Senate, for instance, permits a minority of representatives to postpone or forestall a decision on regulation. While delays are planned to safeguard minority freedoms, they can be employed as a device of obstacle, adding to regulative gridlock.

The strain between the branches, instead of encouraging sound contest, can decline into a condition of unending clash. Leader orders might be utilized to sidestep regulative gridlock, adding to a cycle where each branch looks to dodge the other, disintegrating the cooperative soul planned by the composers of popularity based frameworks.

Finding some kind of harmony among balanced governance and the requirement for proficient administration is a sensitive errand. Changes that upgrade between branch correspondence, support participation, and smooth out dynamic cycles without compromising fundamental oversight components are fundamental. Moreover, tending to procedural devices that can be weaponized for check, like the delay, requires cautious thought to protect minority privileges while forestalling the maltreatment of these systems for sectarian increase.

The Impact of Cash in Legislative issues: Molding Strategy Needs

A guileful underlying issue inside political frameworks is the impact of cash in legislative issues. Crusade supporting, driven by strong vested parties and corporate commitments, presents a layer of intricacy that contorts strategy needs and compromises the honesty of the majority rule process. As monetary interests become laced with political navigation, the components intended to address the desire of individuals can be commandeered by those with the resources to shape the political scene.

The job of cash in legislative issues is especially clear in the US, where the Residents Joined High Court choice opened the conduits for limitless corporate and association spending on political missions. The subsequent deluge of cash has changed political races into high-stakes tries, where competitors depend on monetary help to enhance their messages and gain an upper hand. The results of this monetary reliance are significant, as chosen authorities might focus on the interests of their monetary supporters over the more extensive public great.

Corporate campaigning further fuels the impact of cash in molding strategy results. Campaigning endeavors, energized by significant monetary assets, can influence political choices and needs. Enterprises with critical campaigning power might get strategies that favor their inclinations, regardless of whether those arrangements contradict the prosperity of everybody.

The interlacing of monetary interests with political dynamic trade offs the representativeness of chosen authorities as well as adds to regulative gridlock. Compromise becomes testing when chosen authorities are under obligation to strong vested parties that request relentless help for their positions. This dynamic makes a regulative scene where the interests of the couple of offset the requirements of the many.

Tending to the impact of cash in governmental issues requires a diverse methodology. Crusade finance change is a basic part, requiring measures to restrict the effect of enormous gifts, increment straightforwardness, and lessen the job of cash in forming discretionary results. Stricter guidelines on campaigning, remembering straightforwardness prerequisites and limitations for the rotating entryway among government and campaigning firms, can additionally moderate the excessive impact of monetary interests on strategy choices.

Toward Underlying Changes and Comprehensive Administration

In exploring the conversation on underlying issues inside political frameworks that add to stop, it becomes clear that the ensnarement of these issues shapes an imposing hindrance to compelling administration. Discretionary frameworks, the detachment of abilities, and the impact of cash in governmental issues are not separated factors but rather interconnected components that shape the working of popularity based establishments.

To unwind the gridlock mystery, vital changes are basic. Electing frameworks that offset effortlessness with portrayal, the reasonable recalibration of governing rules to cultivate effective direction, and measures to check the unjustifiable impact of cash in governmental issues are basic parts of an extensive procedure. These changes should be directed by a pledge to inclusivity, straightforwardness, and the standards of majority rule administration.

Additionally, underlying changes ought to be supplemented by endeavors to develop a political culture that values coordinated effort over conflict. Administration that focuses on the benefit of all, rising above partisan principals, and a populace participated in educated and basic talk are fundamental for cultivating a climate where halt is supplanted by unique, responsive administration.

Generally, the conversation on underlying issues inside political frameworks fills in as a source of inspiration. As we wrestle with the intricacies of vote based administration, it becomes obvious that the trap of underlying difficulties requires purposeful and deliberate endeavors to unravel the snare of deterrents ruining powerful direction. Just through a mix of primary changes, social movements, and a restored obligation to the essential standards of a majority rules system might we at any point desire to explore past gridlock toward a political scene that serves the government assistance, everything being equal.

3.3 Examination of partisan polarization, ideological rigidity, and other factors hindering effective governance.

Assessment of Sectarian Polarization, Philosophical Unbending nature, and Different Elements Blocking Viable Administration

In the multifaceted dance of majority rule administration, the peculiarity of hardliner polarization arises as a focal power, using huge impact over the viability of dynamic cycles. Section Three of "Ensnared Gridlock: Disentangling Political Impasse and Easing Human Anguish" dives into the assessment of sectarian polarization, philosophical inflexibility, and different variables that all in all add to the mess of political halt.

Sectarian Polarization: The Augmenting Bay of Political Conflict

At the core of political stop lies the enlarging gap of hardliner polarization, a power that has changed the political scene into a field of philosophical fighting. Sectarian polarization alludes to the dissimilarity of political perspectives and strategy inclinations between individuals from various ideological groups. Instead of participating in helpful discourse and looking for shared belief, political entertainers end up settled in restricting camps, where compromise turns into an uncommon ware.

The underlying foundations of sectarian polarization are profoundly implanted in a complicated exchange of socio-social, financial, and verifiable variables. Issues like race, religion, and social character frequently become caught with political connection, establishing a charged climate where the "us against them" mindset outweighs cooperative critical thinking. The polarization becomes self-supporting as people float towards news sources, groups of friends, and data sources that reverberation their prior convictions, further setting their hardliner personalities.

The results of sectarian polarization are extensive. The regulative cycle, intended to be a discussion for thought and exchange, turns into a milestone where prevailing upon comes first overseeing. Legislators, driven by the basic to fulfill their sectarian base, may focus on scoring political focuses over creating strategies that address the nuanced needs of a different society. The outcome is regulative gridlock, where the quest for philosophical triumphs obscures the basic to resolve major problems.

Moreover, the polarization of political talk stretches out past regulative chambers. Leader activities, legal arrangements, and, surprisingly, the direct of worldwide relations can become prisoner to sectarian contemplations. This polarization can discourage the successful execution of approaches, obstruct worldwide participation, and dissolve the believability of vote based establishments.

Tending to sectarian polarization requires a multi-layered approach. Drives to cultivate a more comprehensive political culture, advance media proficiency, and support cross-party discourse are urgent for moderating the harmful impacts of polarization. Also, discretionary changes that boost control and alliance building, like positioned decision casting a ballot or open primaries, can upset the champ brings home all the glory dynamic that frequently compounds polarization.

Philosophical Unbending nature: The Stronghold of Steadfast Convictions

Firmly interweaved with sectarian polarization is the peculiarity of philosophical inflexibility — a mentality where political entertainers stick undauntedly to a bunch of convictions, frequently to the detriment of practicality and split the difference. Philosophical unbending nature goes about as a stronghold that safeguards people according to elective viewpoints, ruining the adaptability fundamental for compelling administration.

The underlying foundations of philosophical unbending nature can be followed to different sources, including firmly established values, social stories, and party stages. In a climate of energized governmental issues, political entertainers might feel a sense of urgency to adjust to the assumptions for their base, building up a feeling of dedication to philosophical universality. The apprehension about being named as philosophically unclean or a "deceiver" to the reason can establish an environment where deviation from partisan divisions is seen as a disloyalty.

The results of philosophical unbending nature are clear in authoritative chambers where administrators, limited by philosophical imperatives, may dismiss compromise arrangements or bipartisan drives. This determination can bring about authoritative gridlock, leaving basic issues neglected. Additionally, the predominance of philosophical litmus tests in applicant determination can smother variety inside ideological groups, further digging in polarization and repressing the development of imaginative approach arrangements.

Breaking liberated from the shackles of philosophical unbending nature requires a change in political culture that values scholarly adaptability and prizes sober mindedness. Drives to advance cross-party coordinated effort, empower deferential discussion, and perceive the significance of give and take in fair administration are fundamental. Political pioneers who model an eagerness to draw in with restricting perspectives and look for shared view assume a vital part in moving the way of life away from philosophical opinion.

Emergency of Trust: Disintegration of Trust in Organizations

A basic loss from sectarian polarization and philosophical unbending nature is the disintegration of confidence in just foundations. As political entertainers participate in brinkmanship, participate in hyper-hardliner way of talking, and focus on party dependability over the public interest, residents become disappointed with the very establishments intended to address and serve them.

The disintegration of trust appears in different ways. Popular assessments of public sentiment reliably uncover declining trust in regulative bodies, ideological groups, and, surprisingly, the majority rule process itself. The discernment that chosen authorities focus on their own advantages or those of rich contributors over the prosperity of the general population adds to a feeling of disappointment and indifference.

The disintegration of confidence in foundations is a self-building up cycle. As residents withdraw from the political cycle, the variety of voices adding to strategy conversations lessens. This absence of community support further settles in the impact of dug in interests and adds to a criticism circle of disappointment and separation.

Reestablishing trust in establishments requires straightforwardness, responsibility, and a purposeful work to overcome any barrier among residents and their delegates. Hostile to defilement measures, crusade finance changes, and drives to build the availability of the political cycle can assist with remaking trust in the popularity based framework. Furthermore, political pioneers who focus on moral administration and show a promise to serving the public interest assume a crucial part in reestablishing confidence in equitable establishments.

Media Scene: Carefully protected areas and Sentimentality

An essential player in the show of political polarization is the contemporary media scene, described by 24-hour patterns of media reporting, web-based entertainment carefully protected areas, and the prioritization of emotionalism over substance. The media, both conventional and computerized, shapes public discernments, impacts political talk, and assumes a critical part in compounding the difficulties presented by polarization.

The ascent of hardliner media sources and the predominance of calculation driven web-based entertainment takes care of add to the making of data bubbles. People are progressively presented to news and suppositions that line up with their prior convictions, supporting their sectarian characters and limiting comprehension they might interpret complex issues. This carefully protected area impact further settles in philosophical unbending nature and obstructs the potential for useful exchange.

Melodrama, a common element of current media, focuses on sensational stories and polarizing content over nuanced examination. The quest for evaluations and online commitment boosts the enhancement of outrageous perspectives, adding to the polarization of public talk. Issues that request insightful thought and cooperative arrangements are refined into thrilling titles and troublesome ideas, further dissolving the potential for educated and levelheaded public talk.

Tending to the difficulties presented by the media scene requires a blend of media education drives, capable news-casting practices, and endeavors to expand media proprietorship. Media proficiency projects can enable residents to basically assess data sources, perceive among reality and assessment, and explore the perplexing landscape of present day news utilization. Furthermore, drives that advance moral reporting rehearses, reality checking, and a guarantee to introducing different viewpoints add to a more educated and comprehensive public talk.

Social Movements: Sustaining a Governmental issues of Cooperation

As we explore the assessment of variables upsetting powerful administration, it becomes clear that tending to the difficulties presented by hardliner polarization, philosophical unbending nature, the disintegration of trust, and media elements requires more than institutional changes — it requests social movements. Supporting a legislative issues of coordinated effort, inclusivity, and compassion is fundamental for breaking the halt and encouraging a world of politics where the prosperity of residents outweighs sectarian triumphs.

Instructive drives assume a significant part in molding the metro culture. Civics schooling programs that stress the standards of a majority rules government, the significance of give and take, and the worth of community commitment add to an educated and dynamic populace. In equal, drives to advance variety, value, and consideration inside political organizations can reshape the power elements that sustain polarization.

Initiative likewise arises as an impetus for social change. Political pioneers who focus on the benefit of all over hardliner triumphs, take part in conscious and comprehensive exchange, and model a readiness to think twice about a strong model for both their companions and the electorate. By testing the predominant standards of polarization and embracing a governmental issues of coordinated effort, these pioneers add to a social shift that rises above the limits of philosophical unbending nature.

Municipal commitment, worked with by systems that energize the dynamic support of residents in the political cycle, is a foundation of a solid popularity based culture. Drives like participatory planning, municipal events, and deliberative discussions give roads to residents to add to dynamic cycles, cultivating a feeling of pride and organization in the majority rule project.

The assessment of elements ruining successful administration uncovers a perplexing trap of interrelated difficulties. Hardliner polarization, philosophical unbending nature, the disintegration of trust, media elements, and social standards aggregately add to the trap of governmental issues and human affliction. Breaking liberated from this gridlock requests a comprehensive methodology that incorporates institutional changes, media proficiency drives, and social movements. Just through a purposeful work to encourage a governmental issues of joint effort, sympathy, and inclusivity could we at any point desire to explore past the present status of stop and fabricate a political scene that serves the prosperity, everything being equal.

Chapter 4

The Role of Political Leadership

The Job of Political Authority: Exploring Difficulties and Encouraging Compelling Administration

In the midst of the intricacies of majority rule administration, the job of political authority arises as a basic power that can either move a country toward successful administration or propagate the mess of political gridlock. Part Three of "Trapped Gridlock: Disentangling Political Impasse and Mitigating Human Affliction" attempts an investigation of the multi-layered job of political authority, digging into the obligations, challenges, and extraordinary potential that pioneers employ in exploring the complicated elements of current legislative issues.

Authority in a Scene of Gridlock: Difficulties and Goals

Political authority, with regards to dug in gridlock and sectarian polarization, stands up to a novel arrangement of difficulties. The unavoidable philosophical unbending nature that describes contemporary governmental issues frequently represents an impressive deterrent to viable administration. Pioneers wind up exploring a scene where compromise is seen with doubt, and coordinated effort is seen as a treachery of philosophical virtue.

One of the essential difficulties for political innovators in such a scene is the sensitive difficult exercise between party devotion and the basic to oversee for a long term benefit. The strain to adjust to partisan divisions, stick to philosophical conventionality, and take special care of the requests of a sectarian base can make a dynamic where pioneers focus on momentary political increases over the drawn out interests of the country. Exploring this pressure requires an interesting mix of political sharpness, moral boldness, and an unflinching obligation to the standards of majority rule administration.

Besides, the disintegration of confidence in organizations represents a huge obstacle for political pioneers. The thwarted expectation of residents with the political cycle, filled by view of defilement, partisanship, and an absence of responsiveness, requests pioneers who can revamp confidence in fair foundations. The basic to reestablish trust stretches out past simple way of talking; it requires substantial activities that show a promise to straightforwardness, responsibility, and moral administration.

Despite media elements described by melodrama and polarization, political pioneers should fight with the test of discussing successfully with a different and frequently captivated electorate. The 24-hour consistent pattern of media reporting, web-based entertainment closed quarters, and the prioritization of snap commendable stories establish a climate where informing can be mutilated, and political pioneers might end up caught in a pattern of responsive correspondence as opposed to proactive plan setting.

Addressing these difficulties requires an extraordinary way to deal with initiative — one that rises above the constraints of partisanship, embraces a culture of joint effort, and reclassifies achievement not as the loss of political rivals but rather as the headway of the benefit of all. It requests pioneers who can explore the intricacies of a captivated political scene while encouraging a feeling of mutual perspective, inclusivity, and confidence in the vote based process.

The Groundbreaking Capability of Administration: Past Partisanship

While the difficulties are considerable, political authority likewise conveys with it the extraordinary potential to break liberated from the shackles of gridlock and prepare for viable administration. Pioneers who transcend partisanship and focus on the prosperity of their constituents over transient political increases can reshape the political scene and encourage a culture of joint effort.

Fundamental to this extraordinary potential is the capacity of pioneers to show a governmental issues of sympathy and inclusivity. In a captivated climate, where personality governmental issues and philosophical affiliations frequently eclipse shared humankind, pioneers who underline shared belief and celebrate variety become reference points of a more helpful and cooperative political culture.

Initiative that rises above partisanship requires a pledge to exchange and think twice about. As opposed to survey political rivals as enemies to be crushed, pioneers who take part in real discourse cultivate a climate where various viewpoints are thought of, and agreement building turns into a common undertaking. Split the difference, a long way from being an indication of shortcoming, arises as a strength — a demonstration of a pioneer's obligation to tracking down arrangements that address the intricacies of administration.

A groundbreaking chief perceives the significance of moral administration and responsibility. The disintegration of confidence in foundations frequently comes from an impression of debasement and an absence of straightforwardness. Pioneers who focus on moral direct, carry out enemy of defilement measures, and support responsibility convey a strong message that the public interest overshadows individual or hardliner increase.

Besides, a groundbreaking chief grasps the crucial job of community commitment in a sound vote based system. By effectively including residents in the dynamic cycle, pioneers enable people in general to become partners in their administration. Drives like participatory planning, municipal events, and deliberative gatherings give roads to residents to add to strategy conversations, encouraging a feeling of pride and organization in the majority rule project.

In exploring the difficulties of media elements, groundbreaking authority includes becoming the best at compelling correspondence as well as trying the predominant standards of emotionalism and polarization. Pioneers who focus on considerable strategy conversations over title getting manner of speaking, draw in with different news sources, and elevate media proficiency add to a more educated and knowing electorate.

The Basic of Vision: Graphing a Course Past Gridlock

At the core of extraordinary initiative lies the basic of vision — an unmistakable and convincing story that rises above the present status of gridlock and diagrams a course toward a more comprehensive, cooperative, and successful administration. Visionary initiative gives a guide to exploring the intricacies of contemporary governmental issues and motivates residents to take a stab at a superior future by and large.

A groundbreaking vision starts with a profound comprehension of the difficulties confronting society. Pioneers who handle the subtleties of monetary incongruities, social imbalances, and the effect of worldwide difficulties, for example, environmental change can plan arrangements that address the main drivers of human anguish. This understanding goes past philosophical doctrine, expecting pioneers to draw in with proof based arrangements and adjust their methodologies in light of observational real factors.

In making an extraordinary vision, pioneers should express a story that resounds with the different encounters and desires of their constituents. By interfacing with the common upsides of the populace, pioneers make a feeling of aggregate reason that rises above hardliner partitions. This story turns into a bringing together power, cultivating a culture where residents see themselves as members in a common venture instead of as individuals from contradicting camps.

Moreover, a groundbreaking vision perceives the interconnectedness of nearby and worldwide difficulties. In a time of expanding relationship, pioneers who comprehend the worldwide ramifications of their choices can situate their countries as supporters of global participation as opposed to confined entertainers. This worldwide point of view tends to transnational difficulties as well as supports the significance of joint effort chasing shared objectives.

Visionary initiative likewise includes a guarantee to long haul arranging and a dismissal of present moment, politically convenient measures. By focusing on strategies that have getting through benefits, pioneers add to the formation of a steady and practical administration system. This drawn out direction requires political pioneers to endure the tensions of quick political cycles and focus on the prosperity of people in the future.

Developing Extraordinary Administration: The Job of Establishments and Populace

While the extraordinary capability of administration is critical, it is fundamental to perceive that the development of groundbreaking initiative isn't exclusively the obligation of individual pioneers. The job of organizations and the dynamic commitment of the populace assume critical parts in forming a political culture that supports and supports extraordinary initiative.

Institutional systems that boost and award extraordinary authority are vital. Discretionary frameworks, for example, can be intended to energize control and alliance building. Changes, for example, positioned decision casting a ballot or open primaries can upset the champ brings home all the glory dynamic that frequently worsens polarization, making space for pioneers who focus on coordinated effort.

Furthermore, the foundation of moral rules and against defilement estimates inside political establishments supports the assumption for moral direct. Straightforward mission funding guidelines, rigid campaigning limitations, and oversight components add to an administration system where pioneers are considered responsible for their activities and choices.

Residents, as dynamic members in the vote based process, likewise assume a focal part in developing groundbreaking initiative. Educated and drawn in residents add to a political culture that values substance over exhibition, requests responsibility, and prizes pioneers who focus on the benefit of everyone. Media proficiency drives, metro instruction projects, and open doors for community commitment all add to a populace prepared to hold pioneers to exclusive requirements.

Besides, the variety of voices inside the populace adds to a more extravagant embroidery of viewpoints that pioneers can draw upon in making comprehensive strategies. Drives that intensify underestimated voices, advance variety inside political foundations, and address fundamental imbalances make a political scene where pioneers are constrained to think about the necessities, everything being equal.

Generally, the development of groundbreaking initiative is an aggregate undertaking that includes a cooperative connection between pioneers, organizations, and residents. By adjusting institutional motivating forces to the standards of groundbreaking initiative and encouraging a connected with and informed populace, countries can make a political culture that moves chiefs toward powerful administration.

Contextual analyses in Extraordinary Authority: Illustrations Learned

Analyzing contextual investigations of extraordinary initiative gives significant bits of knowledge into the procedures and approaches that pioneers utilize to explore difficulties, break liberated from gridlock, and encourage successful administration. A few models from different political settings offer examples that resound across borders.

Nelson Mandela (South Africa): Nelson Mandela, the notorious head of the counter politically-sanctioned racial segregation development and South Africa's most memorable dark president, exemplified groundbreaking administration even with well established cultural divisions. Mandela's obligation to compromise, pardoning, and inclusivity was instrumental in directing South Africa away from the verge of common difficulty. His accentuation on country working over retaliation added to a serene change to larger part rule, cultivating a feeling of solidarity and common perspective.

Angela Merkel (Germany): Angela Merkel, the Chancellor of Germany, has been a focal figure in European governmental issues and a settling force during seasons of monetary vulnerability. Merkel's administration style, portrayed by realism, joint effort, and a promise to European combination, has situated Germany as a vital participant in foreign relations. Her capacity to explore complex discussions inside the European Association and focus on the drawn out interests of her country has procured her recognition as a groundbreaking chief.

Franklin D. Roosevelt (US): Franklin D. Roosevelt, the 32nd Leader of the US, drove the country through the Economic crisis of the early 20s and The Second Great War. His groundbreaking administration was set apart by intense approach drives, like the New Arrangement, pointed toward addressing financial difficulties and giving help to residents. Roosevelt's capacity to convey a convincing vision, rouse certainty, and adjust to developing conditions exhibits the effect of visionary initiative during seasons of emergency.

Lee Kuan Yew (Singapore): Lee Kuan Yew, the establishing State head of Singapore, is generally viewed as a groundbreaking chief who assumed a crucial part in the country's fast turn of events. Lee's sober minded and trained way to deal with administration zeroed in on financial turn of events, social union, and successful organization. His accentuation on meritocracy, law and order, and upright administration added to Singapore's change from an emerging country to a worldwide monetary center.

These contextual analyses feature the different pathways to extraordinary administration and highlight the significance of context oriented factors. Whether exploring post-politically-sanctioned racial segregation South Africa, controlling Germany through monetary difficulties, driving the US during a time of significant emergency, or changing Singapore into a financial example of overcoming adversity, these pioneers shared normal qualities like a promise to inclusivity, a dream for the future, and a readiness to rise above sectarian partitions.

Toward Extraordinary Administration and Powerful Administration

In exploring the complicated scene of political gridlock, the job of groundbreaking initiative arises as an encouraging sign — a power equipped for breaking the shackles of partisanship, cultivating coordinated effort, and directing countries toward compelling administration. The difficulties are imposing, from settled in philosophical unbending nature to the disintegration of confidence in organizations, however the groundbreaking capability of administration offers a pathway past the present status of gridlock.

Extraordinary initiative requires a guarantee to discourse, inclusivity, and moral administration. Pioneers who transcend hardliner partitions, focus on the benefit of all, and participate in veritable coordinated effort can reshape political societies and move residents to take part in the majority rule project. The basic of vision, grounded in a comprehension of cultural moves and a promise to long haul arranging, turns into the directing power that rises above the constraints of transient political cycles.

Institutional systems that boost and prize extraordinary initiative are significant. Discretionary changes, moral rules, and hostile to defilement measures add to an administration system where pioneers are considered responsible for their activities. Simultaneously, an educated and connected with populace assumes a focal part in molding a political culture that requests responsibility, values joint effort, and prizes pioneers who focus on the government assistance, everything being equal.

The contextual analyses of extraordinary pioneers from assorted settings give important illustrations that resound across borders. Whether exploring complex changes, directing countries through monetary difficulties, or changing social orders, these pioneers shared normal characteristics like compassion, a guarantee to inclusivity, and a dream that rose above quick political contemplations.

As we face the ensnarement of gridlock and human anguish, the basic of extraordinary authority calls. It calls for pioneers who can explore the difficulties of philosophical unbending nature, remake trust in organizations, convey successfully in an enraptured media scene, and art a dream that resounds with the different encounters of their constituents. Through groundbreaking initiative and the aggregate endeavors of organizations and residents, countries can explore past gridlock and fabricate a political scene that serves the prosperity of all.

4.1 Analysis of the impact of political leadership on breaking or perpetuating stalemate.

Examination of the Effect of Political Administration on Breaking or Propagating Impasse

Part Four of "Trapped Gridlock: Unwinding Political Impasse and Easing Human Misery" embraces a complete examination of the urgent job that political initiative plays in one or the other breaking or sustaining the getting through impasses that describe contemporary legislative issues. As we dive into this assessment, we unwind the perplexing elements through which pioneers explore the intricacies of gridlock, impact the direction of political talk, and shape the actual underpinnings of administration.

The Critical Convergence: Political Initiative and Impasse Elements

At the crossing point of political initiative and the steady impasses that plague vote based frameworks lies a sensitive overall influence, impact, and the capacity to explore the tangled difficulties of administration. Impasses, described by regulative gridlock, hardliner polarization, and a disintegration of confidence in establishments, request a nuanced examination of how pioneers, through their activities and choices, either destroy the hindrances to compelling administration or add to the entrapment.

Political pioneers, whether heads of state, party pioneers, or persuasive figures inside political developments, involve a remarkable situation as planners of progress or gatekeepers of business as usual. Their choices shape strategy results, impact the tenor of political talk, and set the vibe for cooperation or conflict inside the corridors of government. Understanding the effect of political initiative on breaking or propagating impasse requires an investigation of key aspects, including vision, coordinated effort, correspondence, and the capacity to explore philosophical partitions.

Visionary Initiative: An Impetus for Breaking Impasse

At the core of extraordinary political initiative lies the force of vision — a convincing story that rises above prompt political contemplations and rouses an aggregate feeling of direction. Visionary pioneers have the capacity to explain a guide for the future, one that reverberates with the goals of the electorate and rises above the dug in divisions that add to impasse.

Visionary authority fills in as an impetus for breaking impasse by giving a reasonable bearing to strategy drives. Even with gridlock, where strategy idleness and sectarian conflicts frequently win, pioneers who articulate a cognizant vision make a story that rises above philosophical unbending nature. This vision turns into a mobilizing point for different partners, cultivating a feeling of common perspective that supports cooperation and split the difference.

One striking illustration of visionary administration breaking impasse is the job of Nelson Mandela in post-politically-sanctioned racial segregation South Africa. Mandela's vision of an accommodated and joined country, enunciated through the idea of the Rainbow Country, filled in as a groundbreaking power that rose above verifiable divisions. His obligation to pardoning and inclusivity gave an establishment to destroying the regulated impasse of politically-sanctioned racial segregation, cultivating another time of administration in light of compromise.

Visionary initiative isn't bound to snapshots of progress; it likewise works as a powerful power inside laid out majority rule governments confronting tireless gridlock. Pioneers who focus on long haul objectives over transient political triumphs articulate a dream that stretches out past electing cycles. Thusly, they challenge the predominant standards of political convenience and add to a political culture that values maintained, principled administration.

Coordinated effort and Agreement Building: Remedys to Gridlock

With regards to political impasse, the capacity of pioneers to cultivate coordinated effort and agreement building arises as a basic determinant of their effect. Impasses frequently result from a breakdown in correspondence, a reluctance to participate in productive exchange, and the prioritization of sectarian triumphs over the benefit of everyone. Pioneers who succeed in joint effort become problem solvers, getting through the obstructions of gridlock by fashioning partnerships and building spans across philosophical partitions.

Fruitful joint effort requires political pioneers to rise above the lose mindset that frequently portrays dug in gridlock. As opposed to review strategy conversations as champ brings home all the glory fights, cooperative pioneers look for mutual benefit arrangements that address the worries of different partners. By focusing on shared values and shared conviction, they establish an environment where compromise isn't seen as shortcoming however as a strength — a pathway to viable administration.

German Chancellor Angela Merkel gives a contemporary illustration of cooperative initiative inside the European setting. Confronting the difficulties of financial vulnerability and the intricacies of European joining, Merkel's initiative style has been set apart by a pledge to cooperative independent direction. Through her capable discussion abilities, she has explored complex European Association elements, fabricated agreement on basic issues, and situated Germany as a balancing out force inside the European structure.

The job of joint effort reaches out past formal political establishments. Pioneers who draw in with common society, include partners in dynamic cycles, and cultivate a culture of inclusivity add to a more lively majority rule government. By perceiving the worth of different viewpoints and effectively looking for input from a wide cluster of voices, cooperative pioneers separate the boundaries that sustain impasse and infuse dynamism into the popularity based process.

Correspondence Systems: Forming Political Talk

Political administration's effect on breaking or propagating impasse is personally attached to correspondence procedures. The capacity of pioneers to actually impart their vision, explore media elements, and draw in with the public shapes the story encompassing strategy drives. In a time of quick data dispersal and elevated polarization, key correspondence turns into a powerful device for pioneers trying to destroy gridlock.

Powerful correspondence includes articulating a convincing vision as well as rising above the closed quarters of hardliner talk. Pioneers who focus on meaningful strategy conversations, draw in with different news sources, and convey in a way that resounds with a wide range of the electorate add to a more educated and connected with populace. By cultivating an environment of open and straight-forward correspondence, they challenge the stories that propagate impasse.

Alternately, pioneers who capitulate to the enticement of sentimentality, partici-pate in disruptive manner of speaking, or focus on transient political additions over meaningful correspondence sustain the elements of gridlock. In a media scene portrayed by polarization and the prioritization of snap commendable satisfied, pioneers who add to the sensationalization of issues ruin the potential for level-headed and informed public talk.

A valid example is the job of media in molding the talk encompassing environ-mental change. Pioneers who utilize key correspondence to convey the desperation of tending to natural difficulties, draw in with logical proof, and cultivate public mindfulness add to breaking the impasse on environment strategy. On the other hand, pioneers who make light of the meaning of ecological issues or take part in falsehood sustain an impasse that blocks progress on basic worldwide difficulties.

Exploring Philosophical Partitions: Sober mindedness and Inclusivity

Political administration's effect on breaking impasse is complicatedly connected to the pioneer's capacity to explore philosophical partitions. In a scene described by sectarian polarization, pioneers who take on a logical methodology and focus on inclusivity become problem solvers. The capacity to rise above unbending phil-osophical limits, fabricate alliances, and oblige assorted points of view cultivates a climate where gridlock is destroyed for cooperative administration.

Commonsense pioneers perceive that powerful administration frequently re-quires split the difference. By recognizing the authentic worries of different part-ners and looking for shared belief, they explore the difficulties of philosophical inflexibility. Sober mindedness doesn't infer a double-crossing of guiding principle but instead an acknowledgment that strategy arrangements should be versatile to the intricacies of administration and receptive to the requirements of a different society.

A prominent model is the initiative of Franklin D. Roosevelt during the New Arrangement period in the US. Confronted with the monetary difficulties of the Economic crisis of the early 20s, Roosevelt took on a down to earth approach that rose above customary philosophical partitions. His organization executed a progres-sion of strategies that drew on both moderate and moderate thoughts, underscoring trial and error and adaptability chasing monetary recuperation.

Inclusivity, as an ally to practicality, includes effectively captivating with different points of view and guaranteeing that the strategy making process mirrors the inter-ests, everything being equal. Pioneers who focus on inclusivity perceive the worth of portrayal and variety inside dynamic bodies. By designating a different scope of consultants, cultivating a culture of open discourse, and effectively looking for input from underestimated voices, comprehensive pioneers challenge the restrictiveness that frequently supports impasse elements.

Interestingly, pioneers who stick unbendingly to philosophical conventionality and focus on sectarian immaculateness add to the propagation of impasse. The refusal to draw in with contradicting perspectives, derision of political rivals, and the burden of litmus tests for party reliability upset the potential for cooperative administration. In such occurrences, the quest for philosophical virtue outweighs the basic to address the complex difficulties confronting society.

Contextual analyses: Administration in Breaking Impasse

Analyzing contextual investigations of political authority gives substantial instances of how pioneers can either break or sustain impasse elements. A few verifiable and contemporary examples offer experiences into the methodologies and approaches that pioneers utilize to explore the intricacies of administration and shape the direction of political talk.

Abraham Lincoln (US): Abraham Lincoln, the sixteenth Leader of the US, gives a convincing contextual investigation of initiative during a basic time of public impasse — the Nationwide conflict. Lincoln's capacity to impart a dream of a rejoined country, explore philosophical partitions, and focus on the benefit of everyone over hardliner interests assumed a crucial part in breaking the impasse of withdrawal. His authority during this turbulent period highlighted the groundbreaking capability of principled and comprehensive initiative.

Margaret Thatcher (Joined Realm): Margaret Thatcher, the primary female State head of the Unified Realm, offers a contextual investigation of initiative during a time of financial and philosophical disturbance. Thatcher's obligation to unregulated economy standards, combined with a down to earth way to deal with administration, assumed a part in breaking the financial impasse of the 1970s. Be that as it may, her administration style likewise added to polarization, as her approaches confronted resistance from different fragments of society.

Justin Trudeau (Canada): Justin Trudeau, the Head of the state of Canada, presents a contemporary contextual investigation of administration in an enraptured political scene. Trudeau's accentuation on inclusivity, variety, and cooperation has been apparent in his way to deal with administration. By designating an orientation adjusted bureau, drawing in with native networks, and advancing social consideration, Trudeau has looked to separate hindrances and cultivate a more comprehensive political culture.

Lee Hsien Loong (Singapore): Lee Hsien Loong, the ongoing State head of Singapore, offers a contextual analysis of authority in a setting where logical administration plays had a focal impact in breaking the impasse of underdevelopment. Singapore's change from a non-industrial country to a worldwide monetary center point under Lee's initiative mirrors the effect of logical arrangements, comprehensive financial methodologies, and a pledge to long haul arranging.

These contextual investigations feature the different procedures utilized by pioneers to break or propagate impasse elements. Whether exploring through nationwide conflict, financial difficulties, political polarization, or the intricacies of a quickly changing worldwide scene, pioneers assume a significant part in forming the direction of their countries. The examples got from these contextual analyses highlight the significance of vision, coordinated effort, correspondence, and exploring philosophical partitions as key components of compelling political administration.

Difficulties to Breaking Impasse: Flexibility and Versatility

While visionary, cooperative, and comprehensive administration can act as an impetus for breaking impasse, pioneers frequently face impressive difficulties in exploring the intricacies of administration. The versatility and flexibility of pioneers notwithstanding these difficulties become basic variables in deciding their effect on breaking or propagating impasse elements.

One inescapable test is the protection from change from settled in interests and laid out power structures. Pioneers upholding for groundbreaking strategies might experience resistance from personal stakes, campaign gatherings, and political adversaries who benefit from the norm. Conquering this opposition requires political expertise as well as the strength to endure pushback and the capacity to prepare public help for change.

The job of hardliner polarization presents another huge test. In conditions where philosophical unbending nature wins, pioneers who try to connect partitions and fabricate agreement might confront interior resistance from inside their own party. The basic to keep up with party solidarity, combined with the gamble of estranging a sectarian base, can ruin pioneers in their endeavors to break impasse. Exploring these inside elements requests a fragile harmony between party dedication and the quest for the benefit of all.

Media elements, portrayed by the 24-hour consistent pattern of media reporting, online entertainment carefully protected areas, and the prioritization of drama, represent extra difficulties to viable administration. Pioneers should battle with the fast spread of data, the mutilation of their messages, and the intensification of troublesome accounts. The capacity to explore media challenges requires versatility in correspondence methodologies, a comprehension of computerized elements, and the ability to draw in with a different scope of news sources.

Besides, the disintegration of confidence in establishments represents an impressive obstruction to pioneers looking to break impasse. Residents disappointed with political cycles and organizations might have some glaring misgivings of pioneers' commitments and drives. Revamping trust requires straightforward and responsible administration as well as a promise to tending to the underlying drivers of doubt, including debasement, saw elitism, and an absence of responsiveness.

Worldwide difficulties, for example, monetary vulnerabilities, general wellbeing emergencies, and natural dangers, add one more layer of intricacy to the authority scene. Pioneers should exhibit flexibility in making arrangements that answer developing worldwide elements. The capacity to explore global relations, team up with different countries, and address transnational difficulties adds to the versatility of pioneers notwithstanding perplexing, interconnected issues.

Administration as the Authority of Progress

In the maze of political impasse, administration arises as the mediator of progress — a power equipped for destroying the obstructions to viable administration or propagating the entanglement of gridlock. The effect of political initiative on breaking or sustaining impasse is certainly not a static or deterministic cycle; it is formed by a complicated interchange of vision, cooperation, correspondence, and flexibility.

Visionary pioneers, drawing on the illustrations of history and the goals of the present, articulate a convincing story that rises above philosophical partitions and moves an aggregate feeling of direction. Their capacity to explore difficulties, encourage joint effort, and impart really shapes the direction of political talk and pushes countries toward viable administration.

Cooperative pioneers, perceiving the interconnectedness of assorted viewpoints, become problem solvers by building spans across philosophical partitions. Through inclusivity, realism, and a promise to discourse, they encourage a political culture that values split the difference and shared arrangements over dug in partisanship.

Correspondence techniques, in the possession of skilled pioneers, become devices for molding public talk, testing disruptive stories, and encouraging an environment of educated and levelheaded exchange. Pioneers who focus on straightforwardness, draw in with different news sources, and convey in a way that reverberates with an expansive range of the electorate add to breaking the impasse on basic issues.

Exploring philosophical partitions requests flexibility and versatility. Pioneers who endure inner and outer tensions, prepare public help for change, and show an ability to address worldwide difficulties add to the extraordinary capability of political initiative.

As we explore the intricacies of contemporary legislative issues, the basic of administration in breaking or propagating impasse calls. In dissecting the effect of political administration, we perceive that the decisions made by pioneers resonate past prompt approach results — they shape the actual groundworks of vote based administration and impact the prosperity of countries. Through visionary, cooperative, and versatile initiative, countries can break liberated from the ensnarement of gridlock and fashion a way toward powerful administration, mitigating human misery and cultivating an all the more and evenhanded society.

4.2 Leaders who successfully navigated through political challenges.

Pioneers Exploring Political Difficulties: Examples from the Intricate Scene

Section Five of "Trapped Gridlock: Unwinding Political Impasse and Mitigating Human Torment" wanders into an itemized investigation of pioneers who, against the background of considerable political difficulties, exhibited strength, vision, and groundbreaking limit. These pioneers, crossing assorted authentic and international settings, offer significant illustrations that rise above time and boundaries. Their accounts enlighten the many-sided elements of authority in the midst of difficulties, giving bits of knowledge into the specialty of exploring political intricacies.

1. **Nelson Mandela: The Draftsman of Compromise**

   Nelson Mandela, the famous head of the counter politically-sanctioned racial segregation development and South Africa's most memorable dark president, remains as a transcending figure in the chronicles of groundbreaking authority. Mandela's process navigated the pot of political battle, detainment, and, at last, the architecting of compromise in a profoundly isolated country.

   Mandela's authority during the wild progress from politically-sanctioned racial segregation to a majority rule government represents the extraordinary capability of flexibility and vision. Even with settled in racial divisions and the danger of common difficulty, Mandela embraced a dream of compromise and inclusivity. His obligation to pardoning and country building turned into the foundation of South Africa's direction toward a bound together and vote based future.

   As a versatile pioneer, Mandela endured 27 years of detainment, arising not disenthralled however with a dream for a country liberated from the shackles of racial mistreatment. His capacity to rise above private misery and channel it into a groundbreaking vision set up for a serene progress.

   The critical illustration from Mandela's administration lies in the groundbreaking force of compromise. In exploring political difficulties, pioneers can draw motivation from Mandela's capacity to transcend harshness, focus on the benefit of everyone, and steer a course toward solidarity. Mandela's heritage provokes pioneers to see compromise not as an indication of shortcoming but rather as a wellspring of solidarity despite firmly established political divisions.

2. **Angela Merkel: Exploring European Difficulties with Practicality**

   Angela Merkel, the Chancellor of Germany, has been a focal figure in European legislative issues during a period set apart by monetary vulnerabilities, relocation emergencies, and difficulties to the European Association's union. Merkel's initiative style, portrayed by sober mindedness, joint effort, and a promise to European combination, offers bits of knowledge into exploring complex international difficulties.

   Confronting the Eurozone emergency, Merkel assumed a critical part in facilitating arrangements and balancing out the European economy. Her logical methodology, accentuating monetary discipline combined with help for battling economies, showed the significance of flexibility despite financial difficulties.

Merkel's authority during the relocation emergency highlighted the meaning of principled sober mindedness. Offsetting helpful worries with the requirement for political security, she pushed for a broad way to deal with address the flood of evacuees. Merkel's readiness to explore the intricacies of movement strategy displayed the significance of initiative that adjusts to developing conditions.

The example from Merkel's administration lies in the viability of practical administration in the midst of international difficulties. Pioneers wrestling with financial vulnerabilities or transnational issues can draw motivation from Merkel's capacity to offset standards with functional arrangements, cultivating dependability and coordinated effort.

3. **Franklin D. Roosevelt: Exploring Emergency with Striking Approach Drives**

Franklin D. Roosevelt, the 32nd Leader of the US, accepted administration during one of the country's most difficult periods — the Economic crisis of the early 20s. Roosevelt's reaction to the monetary emergency, known as the New Arrangement, involved a progression of intense strategy drives pointed toward tending to joblessness, neediness, and financial insecurity.

Roosevelt's authority during the Economic crisis of the early 20s exhibits the extraordinary effect of conclusive activity even with emergency. Through projects, for example, the Works Progress Organization (WPA) and the Government backed retirement Act, Roosevelt executed strategies that expected to ease human misery and give a security net to weak residents.

The example from Roosevelt's authority is the adequacy of striking, extraordinary measures in the midst of emergency. Pioneers facing monetary difficulties or social commotion can draw motivation from Roosevelt's readiness to advance, explore, and focus on the government assistance of residents through definitive arrangement activity.

4. **Lee Kuan Yew: Coordinating Change in Singapore**

Lee Kuan Yew, the establishing State head of Singapore, is credited with coordinating the quick change of the city-state from a non-industrial country to a worldwide monetary force to be reckoned with. Lee's initiative, set apart by sober mindedness, discipline, and a pledge to meritocracy, offers illustrations in country working in the midst of complicated international real factors.

Singapore's process under Lee's initiative represents the extraordinary effect of key administration. Confronted with the difficulties of post-pioneer nationhood, ethnic variety, and monetary underdevelopment, Lee executed arrangements that focused on financial turn of events, social attachment, and viable administration.

The example from Lee's administration lies in the significance of sober minded administration and long haul arranging. Pioneers looking to explore the intricacies of country building can draw motivation from Lee's obligation to meritocracy, law and order, and upright administration as essential components for groundbreaking change.

5. **Abraham Lincoln: Saving the Association In the midst of Nationwide conflict**

Abraham Lincoln, the sixteenth Leader of the US, expected administration during a pivotal occasion in American history — the Nationwide conflict. Lincoln's administration, described by a promise to saving the Association and tending to the ethical test of bondage, offers persevering through illustrations in exploring the intricacies of political emergencies.

Lincoln's administration displayed the extraordinary capability of principled authority in the midst of significant division. His Liberation Declaration and the Gettysburg Address highlighted a guarantee to equity and correspondence, molding the direction of American history.

The illustration from Lincoln's administration is the persevering through effect of principled administration. Pioneers defying significant moral difficulties or cultural divisions can draw motivation from Lincoln's resolute obligation to the standards of a majority rules system and equity, even notwithstanding existential dangers to the country.

6. **Winston Churchill: Administration Notwithstanding The Second Great War**

Winston Churchill, the State head of the Unified Realm during The Second Great War, arose as an image of strength, assurance, and groundbreaking administration despite worldwide clash. Churchill's administration during quite possibly of the most obscure period in present day history offers bits of knowledge into exploring international difficulties with fortitude and vital keenness.

Churchill's discourses, for example, the popular "We will battle on the sea shores" address, embody the extraordinary force of motivational authority. His capacity to mobilize the English public and the United powers, even in the haziest hours of the conflict, exhibited the significance of correspondence in molding public determination.

The example from Churchill's administration is the effect of motivational authority in the midst of emergency. Pioneers confronting international difficulties or worldwide contentions can draw motivation from Churchill's capacity to give vision, versatility, and a feeling of direction to a country facing existential dangers.

7. **Justin Trudeau: Contemporary Administration in a Captivated Scene**

Justin Trudeau, the State head of Canada, gives a contemporary contextual investigation of authority in an energized political scene. Trudeau's initiative, set apart by an accentuation on inclusivity, variety, and cooperation, offers bits of knowledge into exploring contemporary difficulties with an emphasis on friendly union.

Trudeau's obligation to orientation correspondence, variety, and compromise with native networks grandstands the groundbreaking capability of comprehensive administration. By naming an orientation adjusted bureau, drawing in with minimized networks, and supporting moderate strategies, Trudeau has looked to address verifiable imbalances and encourage a more comprehensive political culture.

The illustration from Trudeau's administration is the effect of focusing on inclusivity and variety. Pioneers wrestling with cultural divisions or trying to address verifiable treacheries can draw motivation from Trudeau's accentuation on making a political culture that esteems the commitments, everything being equal.

Core values for Explore Political Difficulties

As we dig into the tales of pioneers who effectively explored political difficulties, a few core values arise, giving a guide to current and future pioneers confronting complex political scenes.

Flexibility as a Wellspring of Change: The pioneers analyzed, from Nelson Mandela to Winston Churchill, showed noteworthy strength even with misfortune. Versatility turns into a wellspring of extraordinary authority, empowering pioneers to endure difficulties, keep a feeling of direction, and arise more grounded chasing their vision.

Visionary Administration In the midst of Emergency: Visionary pioneers, like Mandela, Roosevelt, and Lincoln, exhibited the groundbreaking effect of articulating an unmistakable vision in the midst of emergency. A convincing vision turns into a mobilizing point for residents, cultivating solidarity and giving a guide to exploring through difficulties.

Practicality and Flexibility: Pioneers like Angela Merkel and Lee Kuan Yew exhibited the significance of realism and versatility in administration. Exploring political provokes expects pioneers to be adaptable, able to improve, and skilled at tracking down useful answers for complex issues.

Comprehensive Administration for Social Attachment: Pioneers like Justin Trudeau highlight the extraordinary capability of comprehensive administration in cultivating social union. Focusing on inclusivity, variety, and tending to verifiable disparities become fundamental components in building a political culture that esteems the commitments, all things considered.

Compelling Correspondence as an Initiative Device: Churchill's wartime talks and Trudeau's correspondence systems feature the significance of successful correspondence in initiative. Pioneers should be capable at conveying their vision, mobilizing public help, and molding public talk, especially in the midst of emergency.

Principled Administration Even with Moral Difficulties: Lincoln's principled position on subjugation represents the extraordinary effect of principled authority notwithstanding upright difficulties. Pioneers facing significant moral problems should draw strength from resolute obligation to majority rule standards and equity.

Motivation as an Impetus for Change: Churchill's helpful authority during The Second Great War shows the groundbreaking force of moving residents in the midst of emergency. Pioneers can catalyze change by giving a feeling of motivation, strength, and a dream for a superior future.

In exploring the entrapped gridlock of contemporary legislative issues, pioneers can find direction in these standards got from the tales of extraordinary authority. The difficulties might change — from financial emergencies to social divisions, from international contentions to worldwide pandemics — however the standards of versatility, vision, flexibility, inclusivity, compelling correspondence, principled administration, and motivation stay ageless. As pioneers diagram their course through the mind boggling scene of political difficulties, the examples from these extraordinary pioneers act as reference points of shrewdness, offering experiences into the craft of exploring the unpredictable elements of administration and directing countries toward an additional fair and evenhanded future.

4.3 Exploration of the qualities and strategies necessary for effective leadership in overcoming gridlock.

Investigation of Characteristics and Systems for Powerful Administration in Conquering Gridlock

Part Six of "Entrapped Gridlock: Disentangling Political Impasse and Reducing Human Affliction" leaves on a top to bottom investigation of the fundamental characteristics and systems vital for powerful administration in the difficult landscape of conquering gridlock. Despite dug in political divisions, regulative impasses, and cultural strife, pioneers should exemplify a remarkable arrangement of qualities and utilize vital ways to deal with get through the hindrances upsetting powerful administration. This investigation digs into the diverse idea of authority, divulging the groundbreaking possible that lies in characteristics like vision, cooperation, versatility, and moral administration.

Visionary Initiative: Graphing a Course Past Partisanship

At the core of successful initiative in beating gridlock lies visionary prescience — an ability to verbalize a convincing and comprehensive vision that rises above sectarian partitions. Visionary pioneers have the capacity to transcend quick political contemplations and proposition a guide that reverberates with the more extensive desires of the electorate. This ability to explain a binding together story turns into a strong power in getting through the entrapment of gridlock.

A valid example is Nelson Mandela's visionary authority in post-politically-sanctioned racial segregation South Africa. Mandela's vision of an accommodated country, embodied in the idea of the Rainbow Country, filled in as a directing light in guiding the country away from the edge of common conflict. His obligation to pardoning and inclusivity turned into the impetus for destroying systematized grid-lock and cultivating another time of administration.

Powerful forerunners notwithstanding gridlock should copy Mandela's capacity to rise above quick political contemplations and well-spoken a dream that resounds with the shared perspective of the general public. This visionary methodology turns into an extension that traverses philosophical partitions, making a shared belief for different partners to mobilize behind shared objectives.

Cooperative Authority: Producing Coalitions Past Sectarian Lines

Gridlock frequently flourishes with the ill-disposed nature of political talk, where philosophical inflexibility overshadows cooperative critical thinking. Pioneers ready to beat gridlock should epitomize cooperative initiative, utilizing the specialty of building partnerships and encouraging participation across sectarian lines. In the cauldron of gridlock, coordinated effort turns into an essential objective, empowering pioneers to get through the logjam of settled in places.

The authority of Angela Merkel, especially during the Eurozone emergency, embodies cooperative administration. Merkel's proficient exchange abilities and obligation to settling on something worth agreeing on inside the European Association added to balancing out the monetary difficulties confronting the landmass. Her capacity to fashion partnerships and explore complex international elements highlighted the extraordinary capability of cooperative initiative.

Pioneers looking to beat gridlock should embrace a cooperative mentality that focuses on shared objectives over individual triumphs. By encouraging an environment of collaboration, pioneers can connect philosophical partitions, fabricate agreement on basic issues, and usher in another time of administration described by powerful critical thinking.

Versatile Initiative: Exploring Intricacy with Adaptability

Gridlock frequently emerges because of the failure of political frameworks to adjust to advancing difficulties and evolving conditions. Successful pioneers should epitomize versatile initiative — an ability to explore intricacy with adaptability, development, and a readiness to embrace change. Notwithstanding quickly moving political scenes, flexibility turns into a key part for getting through gridlock and controlling administration toward powerful arrangements.

Franklin D. Roosevelt's initiative during the Economic crisis of the early 20s gives a demonstration of the extraordinary effect of versatile administration. Confronted with extraordinary monetary difficulties, Roosevelt executed strong and inventive strategies under the New Arrangement, exhibiting the ability to adjust to the requests existing apart from everything else. His adaptability in administration became instrumental in resolving the multi-layered issues of the time.

Pioneers standing up to gridlock should draw motivation from Roosevelt's versatile initiative, perceiving that powerful administration requires a readiness to develop, try, and adjust to the intricacies of the cutting edge world. By embracing change and exhibiting adaptability, pioneers can explore through the entrapment of gridlock and answer actually to the advancing necessities of their social orders.

Moral Administration: Reconstructing Confidence in Organizations

One of the hidden reasons for gridlock is much of the time an unavoidable disintegration of confidence in political foundations. Successful forerunners in defeating gridlock should focus on moral administration — a faithful obligation to straightforwardness, responsibility, and the genuinely honorable best expectations. By revamping trust in organizations, pioneers can cultivate a climate helpful for joint effort and viable administration.

The groundbreaking authority of Lee Kuan Yew in Singapore gives a contextual analysis in moral administration. Lee's obligation to meritocracy, law and order, and honest administration assumed a vital part in Singapore's fast change. His accentuation on moral standards turned into a foundation for building trust in organizations, guaranteeing the solidness vital for successful administration.

Pioneers looking to get through gridlock should focus on moral administration as a fundamental component of their initiative. Straightforward navigation, responsibility for activities, and a guarantee to maintaining the most noteworthy moral norms become fundamental parts in remaking the trust of residents and establishing a favorable climate for cooperative administration.

Comprehensive Initiative: Intensifying Assorted Viewpoints

Gridlock is in many cases exacerbated by an absence of inclusivity inside the political dynamic cycle. Viable pioneers should embrace comprehensive initiative — a promise to enhancing different viewpoints, connecting with minimized voices, and guaranteeing that the policymaking system mirrors the interests, everything being equal. Inclusivity turns into a strong cure to the exclusionary elements that add to gridlock.

Justin Trudeau's authority in Canada offers experiences into the extraordinary capability of comprehensive administration. Trudeau's accentuation on orientation fairness, variety, and compromise with native networks highlights the significance of making a political culture that esteems the commitments, everything being equal. His obligation to inclusivity has turned into a main impetus in molding a more dynamic and cooperative vote based system.

Pioneers looking to beat gridlock should focus on inclusivity as a core value in their initiative. By effectively captivating with different viewpoints, including partners in dynamic cycles, and tending to foundational imbalances, pioneers can make a political scene where the necessities of all residents are thought of, encouraging a more comprehensive and compelling administration.

Viable Correspondence: Molding the Story for Cooperation

Correspondence is a key part in the authority tool stash for defeating gridlock. Compelling pioneers should excel at correspondence, forming the story such that encourages coordinated effort, disperses polarization, and connects with residents in the majority rule process. In a media scene set apart by polarization and sentimentality, vital correspondence turns into a groundbreaking power for getting through the boundaries of gridlock.

Winston Churchill's initiative during The Second Great War gives a convincing illustration of the groundbreaking force of compelling correspondence. Churchill's discourses, set apart by expressiveness and helpful informing, mobilized the English public and the Associated powers during quite possibly of the most obscure period in current history. His capacity to shape the story turned into an essential resource in preparing support for a typical reason.

Pioneers standing up to gridlock should perceive the significance of successful correspondence in molding public talk. By focusing on straightforwardness, drawing in with different news sources, and imparting in a way that reverberates with a wide range of the electorate, pioneers can challenge disruptive stories and encourage an environment of educated and objective exchange.

Valiant Authority: Defying Disagreeable Real factors

Beating gridlock frequently expects pioneers to face disliked real factors, go with hard decisions, and stir things up. Gallant initiative — an eagerness to handle petulant issues, address well established issues, and seek after fundamental changes — turns into a sign of extraordinary administration. Pioneers should exemplify the fortitude to explore through political disturbance and move toward powerful arrangements.

Abraham Lincoln's initiative during the Nationwide conflict gives a strong illustration of fearless authority. Defied with the ethical test of subjection and the existential danger to the Association, Lincoln showed the fortitude to establish the Liberation Declaration and seek after approaches focused on equity and fairness. His readiness to face disagreeable real factors turned into an impetus for groundbreaking change.

Pioneers trying to beat gridlock should show the fortitude to defy disruptive issues, challenge dug in interests, and seek after strategies that might confront obstruction. By focusing on the benefit of all over momentary political additions, pioneers can make a plan toward powerful administration, even despite misfortune.

Key Independent direction: Adjusting Present moment and Long haul Objectives

Compelling forerunners in conquering gridlock should succeed in essential navigation — an ability to adjust transient political contemplations with long haul objectives. In the pot of gridlock, where quick hardliner triumphs frequently come first, pioneers should embrace an essential methodology that focuses on supported and principled administration over temporary victories.

Angela Merkel's initiative during the Eurozone emergency features the extraordinary effect of vital direction. Merkel's accentuation on monetary discipline combined with help for battling economies exhibited a nuanced comprehension of the requirement for both transient solidness and long haul financial manageability. Her essential methodology added to settling the European economy during a time of significant vulnerability.

Pioneers wrestling with gridlock should focus on essential decision-production as a focal component of their initiative. By taking on a drawn out point of view, underscoring principled administration, and exploring the intricacies of administration with key insight, pioneers can get through the trap of gridlock and set a direction toward maintained and powerful administration.

An Outline for Groundbreaking Initiative

In exploring the difficult scene of gridlock, pioneers should encapsulate a complex arrangement of characteristics and utilize key methodologies that address the main drivers of political impasse. Visionary premonition, cooperative administration, flexibility, moral standards, inclusivity, successful correspondence, gallant independent direction, and vital keenness by and large structure a diagram for extraordinary initiative.

As pioneers outline their course through the ensnared gridlock of contemporary legislative issues, the examples drawn from Mandela, Merkel, Roosevelt, Lee, Lincoln, Churchill, Trudeau, and others offer a rich embroidery of bits of knowledge. The investigation of these characteristics and methodologies enlightens the extraordinary expected that exists in the grip of pioneers ready to rise above prompt political contemplations and focus on the benefit of all.

In the embroidery of successful administration, the strings of vision, cooperation, flexibility, moral administration, inclusivity, powerful correspondence, boldness, and key dynamic wind around together to make a story of groundbreaking change. Pioneers who embrace these characteristics become designers of administration fit for getting through gridlock, encouraging cooperation, and setting countries on a course toward successful and principled administration.

In the fantastic embroidery of extraordinary authority, the strings of vision, coordinated effort, flexibility, moral administration, inclusivity, powerful correspondence, fortitude, and key dynamic wind around together to make a story of groundbreaking change. Pioneers who embrace these characteristics become planners of administration equipped for getting through gridlock, cultivating joint effort, and setting countries on a course toward powerful and principled administration.

Chapter 5

Global Perspectives on Political Stalemate

Worldwide Points of view on Political Impasse: Unwinding the Perplexing Woven artwork

Part Seven of "Entrapped Gridlock: Disentangling Political Impasse and Mitigating Human Misery" digs into a complete investigation of worldwide viewpoints on political impasse. As political scenes develop and entwine on a worldwide scale, understanding the different indications and shared difficulties of political gridlock becomes vital. This section investigates how countries across mainlands wrestle with issues of administration, polarization, and the effect of political gridlock on social orders in general.

1. **European Association: Exploring Solidarity and Disparity**

   The European Association (EU) remains as an exceptional contextual investigation in worldwide governmental issues, exhibiting both the conceivable outcomes and difficulties of multi-country administration. The EU's complex political design, portrayed by shared power and various public interests, frequently experiences political impasse in dynamic cycles. As part states explore the fragile harmony among solidarity and public independence, issues like monetary arrangements, movement, and institutional changes can become wellsprings of dispute.

   The Eurozone emergency fills in as an impactful illustration of political impasse inside the EU. As part states with differing financial interests wrestled with the monetary slump, arriving at agreement on monetary arrangements demonstrated testing. The strain between nations supporting for grimness measures and those underlining improvement bundles featured the intricacies of dynamic inside the EU structure.

   The advancing idea of political coalitions, for example, the Visegrád

Gathering's position on relocation arrangements, further highlights the difficulties of accomplishing agreement. While some part states underline public sway in deciding movement strategies, others advocate for a more bound together and composed approach. This variety of points of view frequently adds to political gridlock inside the EU, mirroring the many-sided embroidered artwork of shared administration and public independence.

2. **US: Polarization and Official Stop**

The US, a signal of a vote based system, has wrestled with expanding political polarization, prompting regulative gridlock and administration challenges. The two-party situation, described by philosophical unbending nature and sectarian partitions, has frequently ruined the entry of key regulation. Issues, for example, medical care change, movement, and environmental change alleviation have become landmarks where political impasse wins.

The peculiarity of delaying in the U.S. Senate epitomizes the procedural instruments that add to official gridlock. The capacity of a minority party to draw out discusses and hinder dynamic cycles enhances the difficulties of arriving at agreement. The repercussions of such gridlock stretch out past homegrown arrangement, influencing the country's capacity to answer really to worldwide difficulties.

The antagonistic idea of affirmation processes for key arrangements, including High Court judges, further represents how political polarization can hinder the working of imperative foundations. The battle to accomplish bipartisan help for candidates frequently prompts delayed opening and hampers the legal executive's ability to satisfy its job as a beware of leader and regulative power.

3. **India: Alliance Legislative issues and Strategy Gridlock**

India, with its dynamic majority rules government and multiparty framework, gives experiences into the difficulties of alliance legislative issues and its effect on administration. The need of shaping alliances to get a parliamentary larger part frequently brings about different gatherings with changing strategy needs meeting up. While alliance states mirror the pluralistic idea of Indian majority rule government, they additionally present difficulties as far as strategy coordination and navigation.

Strategy gridlock in India is many times exacerbated by territorial and collective interests, as various gatherings inside an alliance advocate for arrangements that line up with their citizen bases. Financial changes, framework advancement, and social government assistance programs are among the areas where disparate strategy inclinations can prompt difficulties in execution.

The requirement for agreement building and split the difference in an alliance driven political scene presents intrinsic difficulties. While alliance state run administrations can unite assorted voices, the journey for agreement might bring about arrangement choices that are weakened or postponed. Adjusting the interests of different alliance accomplices turns into a fragile errand for pioneers, frequently adding to political impasse.

4. **China: Tyrant Solidness and Strategy Coherence**

China's political scene, described by a one-party framework and tyrant administration, stands out distinctly from the multiparty popular governments examined before. While China doesn't confront similar difficulties of hardliner gridlock, its political framework isn't insusceptible to its own intricacies, including the requirement for strategy coherence and flexibility.

The incorporated idea of dynamic inside the Chinese Socialist Coalition (CCP) takes into consideration quick strategy execution, encouraging monetary turn of events and framework projects. In any case, the absence of a multiparty framework and open political contest can restrict the variety of points of view in strategy detailing. The shortfall of a vigorous arrangement of balanced governance likewise presents difficulties in resolving issues of debasement and responsibility.

China's way to deal with political steadiness and financial advancement brings up issues about the compromises between compelling administration and popularity based standards. The congruity in strategy course worked with by the CCP has added to quick monetary development, yet it additionally raises worries about political opportunities, basic liberties, and public support in direction.

5. **Brazil: Political Choppiness and Administration Difficulties**

Brazil's political scene gives a focal point through which to look at the effect of political disturbance on administration. Times of political insecurity, including reprimand procedures and debasement outrages, have added to strategy gridlock and thwarted compelling administration. The difficulties of exploring a complex political landscape feature the significance of institutional strength and the capacity to address defilement inside political designs.

The denunciation of two Brazilian presidents as of late, Dilma Rousseff and Michel Temer, highlights the effect of political precariousness on administration. The course of denunciation, while an established system, can prompt extended political fights and ruin the execution of key strategies. The subsequent gridlock presents difficulties for resolving major problems, including monetary changes and social government assistance programs.

Defilement outrages, for example, those including the state-controlled oil organization Petrobras, further confound the political scene. The need to address debasement inside political foundations turns into a pivotal part of viable administration. Adjusting the goals of responsibility with the requirement for strategy congruity represents a one of a kind arrangement of difficulties for pioneers in Brazil.

6. **South Africa: Progress and Change**

South Africa's excursion from politically-sanctioned racial segregation to a majority rule government gives a convincing contextual investigation of political progress and the difficulties of changing a profoundly partitioned society. The post-politically-sanctioned racial segregation time, set apart by endeavors to accomplish compromise and address verifiable shameful acts, offers experiences into the intricacies of administration in the repercussions of fundamental persecution.

Reality and Compromise Commission (TRC), laid out to address common liberties infringement during politically-sanctioned racial segregation, reflects South Africa's obligation to temporary equity. In any case, the fragile harmony among equity and compromise presents continuous difficulties for administration. The need to address financial disparities, land change, and political portrayal further highlights the intricacies of post-politically-sanctioned racial segregation administration.

South Africa's experience features the significance of comprehensive administration in the fallout of political progress. The basic to incorporate different voices, address verifiable treacheries, and encourage social union becomes integral to successful administration. In any case, the mission for agreement on groundbreaking approaches frequently experiences difficulties, adding to political impasse.

7. **Center East: Territorial Contentions and Administration Difficulties**

The Center East, described by complex international elements and territorial contentions, presents an exceptional arrangement of difficulties for successful administration. The transaction of partisan strains, international competitions, and authentic complaints has added to political shakiness and administration challenges in the area.

Nations like Iraq, Syria, and Lebanon have confronted delayed times of political disturbance, including equipped struggles and outer intercessions. The effect of such insecurity on administration is significant, with issues of state-building, reproduction, and social attachment becoming vital to the political scene.

The difficulties of tending to territorial contentions, obliging different ethnic and strict networks, and building stable political organizations highlight the intricacies of administration in the Center East. The interconnected idea of international elements in the locale further enhances the difficulties of successful administration, frequently prompting political impasse on major questions.

Illustrations according to Worldwide Viewpoints

The worldwide viewpoints on political impasse introduced in this part highlight the assorted difficulties and shared intricacies that countries face in the domain of administration. Whether exploring the complexities of alliance governmental issues in India, tending to polarization in the US, or overseeing territorial struggles in the Center East, pioneers wrestle with the basic of viable administration notwithstanding different political scenes.

From the complexities of the European Association's common administration to the difficulties of tyrant strength in China, each worldwide viewpoint offers one of a kind experiences into the elements of political impasse. The examples drawn from these assorted settings feature the significance of flexibility, inclusivity, moral administration, and key dynamic in conquering the ensnarement of gridlock.

As countries endeavor to unwind political impasse and reduce human misery, the worldwide points of view inspected in this part act as an aggregate embroidery of encounters, difficulties, and illustrations. The intricacy of administration rises above borders, and the requirement for groundbreaking initiative turns into an all inclusive goal. By drawing on the experiences acquired according to worldwide points of view, pioneers can explore the complicated elements of political scenes and produce a way toward compelling and principled administration.

5.1 Comparative analysis of political stalemates in different regions of the world.

Near Investigation of Political Impasses: Disentangling Territorial Elements

This part participates in a thorough near examination of political impasses in various locales of the world. As political scenes shift altogether across landmasses, understanding the one of a kind difficulties and shared examples of political gridlock becomes fundamental. The assessment of political impasses in Europe, North America, Asia, Africa, and Latin America reveals nuanced territorial elements, revealing insight into the basic variables adding to administration challenges.

1. **Europe: The Mind boggling Embroidery of Shared Sway**

   The European landmass, known for its different social scene and verifiable intricacies, wrestles with an exceptional type of political impasse inside the structure of the European Association (EU). The EU's trial with shared power and multi-country administration presents the two amazing open doors for coordinated effort and difficulties in navigation.

   The Eurozone emergency, a financial slump that impacted a few part states, displayed the intricacies of accomplishing agreement on monetary strategies. Dissimilar financial interests and the strain between somberness measures and improvement bundles featured the hardships of exploring monetary difficulties inside a structure that requests solidarity yet saves public independence.

   The issue of movement strategy further highlighted the difficulties of accommodating assorted public interests inside the EU. The Visegrád Gathering's protection from a brought together methodology, pushing for individual sway in deciding migration strategies, displayed the sensitive harmony between aggregate direction and public independence.

The relative examination of political impasses in Europe accentuates the many-sided embroidery of shared administration. As countries explore the difficulties of coordinated effort and public interests inside the EU structure, the locale gives bits of knowledge into the intricacies of decision-production in a multi-country setting.

2. **North America: Polarization and Institutional Difficulties**

North America, with its different political frameworks and monetary forces to be reckoned with, faces particular difficulties connected with political impasses. The US, described by a two-party framework and expanding polarization, wrestles with regulative stop that blocks viable administration.

The peculiarity of delaying in the U.S. Senate fills in as a procedural component adding to political gridlock. The capacity of a minority party to draw out discusses and impede dynamic cycles worsens the difficulties of arriving at agreement on basic issues, for example, medical services change, movement, and environmental change relief.

The affirmation processes for key arrangements, including High Court judges, further epitomize the effect of political polarization on institutional working. Delayed opening and disagreeable fights over chosen people feature the hardships of accomplishing bipartisan help and guaranteeing the legal executive's powerful job as a beware of different parts of government.

The near examination of political impasses in North America underlines the difficulties presented by a two-party framework and developing philosophical divisions. The mind boggling elements of regulative halt and the effect on institutional soundness give important bits of knowledge into the district's administration challenges.

3. **Asia: Alliance Legislative issues and Fast Change**

The Asian mainland, home to different political frameworks and monetary forces to be reckoned with, wrestles with political impasses molded by elements like alliance legislative issues and fast change. India, with its multiparty a majority rules system, gives a captivating contextual investigation of administration challenges emerging from the need of shaping alliances.

Alliance governmental issues in India, while mirroring the pluralistic idea of its majority rules system, presents difficulties as far as strategy coordination and direction. Dissimilar strategy inclinations among alliance accomplices, driven by provincial and collective interests, add to difficulties in executing key arrangements connected with financial changes, foundation advancement, and social government assistance programs.

China's one-party framework and dictator administration, then again, exhibit an alternate arrangement of difficulties connected with political strength and strategy progression. While the unified navigation takes into consideration quick arrangement execution, the absence of political pluralism raises worries about variety of viewpoints and issues of responsibility.

The near examination of political impasses in Asia features the assorted difficulties emerging from alliance governmental issues and tyrant administration. The exchange of political frameworks and the effect on strategy plan and execution give a nuanced comprehension of administration elements in the locale.

4. **Africa: Change, Change, and Steady Difficulties**

The African mainland, set apart by different narratives and post-frontier challenges, goes through changes and changes that shape its political scene. South Africa's excursion from politically-sanctioned racial segregation to a vote based system gives a convincing contextual investigation of political impasses emerging from the requirement for cultural change.

The post-politically-sanctioned racial segregation period in South Africa, while set apart by endeavors to accomplish compromise and address verifiable shameful acts through systems like Reality and Compromise Commission (TRC), faces continuous difficulties. The basic to address financial disparities, land change, and political portrayal highlights the intricacies of post-politically-sanctioned racial segregation administration.

The similar examination of political impasses in Africa underlines the steady difficulties emerging from authentic heritages, post-provincial changes, and the basic of groundbreaking administration. The sensitive harmony among equity and compromise, as found in South Africa, offers significant experiences into the intricacies of administration in the area.

5. **Latin America: Choppiness, Defilement, and Administration Battles**

The Latin American mainland, described by different political frameworks and financial inconsistencies, wrestles with political choppiness, debasement, and administration battles. Brazil's political scene, set apart by indictment procedures and defilement embarrassments, gives a focal point through which to look at the effect of political precariousness on administration.

The denunciation of Brazilian presidents, like Dilma Rousseff and Michel Temer, features the difficulties of administration in the midst of political choppiness. The extended political fights and issues connected with defilement inside political foundations add to strategy gridlock and upset the execution of key changes.

The relative examination of political impasses in Latin America highlights the effect of political disturbance and defilement on administration. The battles to offset responsibility with the basic of strategy congruity give important experiences into the intricacies of administration in the area.

Disentangling Examples and Spanning Partitions

The relative examination of political impasses across various locales offers an all encompassing perspective on the intricacies, difficulties, and examples that characterize administration elements. From the common sway battles in Europe to the polarization challenges in North America, and from the alliance legislative issues in Asia to the groundbreaking administration battles in Africa and Latin America, every district presents an extraordinary embroidery of administration challenges.

Designs arise, uncovering the effect of political frameworks, verifiable inheritances, and cultural changes on the idea of political impasses. The sensitive harmony between public independence and shared administration, the difficulties presented by polarization and extending philosophical partitions, and the basic of groundbreaking administration in post-provincial settings become focal topics in the near examination.

As countries wrestle with political impasses, connecting partitions and figuring out something worth agreeing on arise as objectives for successful administration. The illustrations drawn from different areas highlight the significance of flexibility, inclusivity, moral administration, and vital direction. By unwinding the territorial elements of political impasses, pioneers can gather significant experiences to explore the perplexing woven artwork of administration difficulties and steer their countries toward viable and principled administration.

5.2 Examination of successful models for resolving political gridlock in various countries.

Assessment of Effective Models for Settling Political Gridlock: Examples from Worldwide Authority

In the steadily developing scene of worldwide administration, the assessment of fruitful models for settling political gridlock remains as an encouraging sign and motivation. This part digs into assorted contextual investigations from different nations, revealing groundbreaking methodologies and administration procedures that have successfully gotten through the trap of political impasse. From cooperative decision-production to imaginative institutional changes, these models offer important illustrations for pioneers looking to explore the intricacies of administration and cultivate compelling, principled authority.

1. **Germany: The Alliance Agreement Model**

    Germany, prestigious for its steady and cooperative administration, gives a convincing model to settling political gridlock through the Alliance Agreement approach. The German political framework, described by corresponding portrayal and a multiparty scene, frequently requires alliance states to get a greater part in the Bundestag.

    The alliance agreement model depends on the craft of exchange and split the difference among ideological groups with assorted philosophical foundations. Pioneers in Germany, especially Chancellor Angela Merkel, have adroitly explored alliance elements, fashioning arrangements that focus on shared objectives over hardliner interests. The accentuation on agreement building guarantees that key strategies mirror a wide range of viewpoints, encouraging soundness and powerful administration.

Merkel's authority during the Eurozone emergency epitomizes the progress of the alliance agreement model. By encouraging cooperation among alliance accomplices and European partners, Merkel assumed a significant part in balancing out the financial difficulties confronting the mainland. The accentuation on agreement and compromise became instrumental in defeating the gridlock that frequently goes with complex monetary choices.

2. **Singapore: Down to earth Administration and Technocratic Authority**

Singapore, a little however financially strong country, offers a model of settling political gridlock through realistic administration and technocratic initiative. The initiative of Lee Kuan Yew, the principal architect of present day Singapore, represents a model that focuses on long haul arranging, key navigation, and an emphasis on technocratic skill.

The sober minded administration model in Singapore is set apart by an outcomes situated approach, where strategies are executed in view of observational proof and a sharp comprehension of cultural necessities. Lee Kuan Yew's obligation to meritocracy, straightforwardness, and a productive common help turned into the foundation of Singapore's fast change from a non-industrial country to a worldwide financial force to be reckoned with.

The technocratic administration in Singapore puts accentuation on the mastery of experts in policymaking. By depending on a framework of exceptionally taught and talented people, the public authority guarantees that choices are grounded in specialized capability, encouraging viable administration. This approach limits philosophical gridlock, considering quick and informed independent direction.

3. **Canada: Comprehensive Administration and Social Attachment**

Canada's model for settling political gridlock fixates on comprehensive administration and the advancement of social attachment. With its assorted and multicultural society, Canada has effectively explored political difficulties by focusing on inclusivity, variety, and compromise with native networks.

Pioneers, for example, Justin Trudeau have embraced comprehensive administration, underscoring the significance of intensifying assorted voices and tending to verifiable treacheries. Trudeau's obligation to orientation correspondence, multiculturalism, and civil rights has added to a political culture that esteems the commitments, everything being equal, limiting the gamble of gridlock emerging from exclusionary strategies.

Reality and Compromise Commission in Canada remains as an extraordinary drive, tending to verifiable treacheries against native networks. By participating in a course of truth-chasing and recognizing past wrongs, Canada embodies a model for conquering gridlock established in verifiable complaints. The obligation to social union turns into a main thrust in building a more comprehensive and successful administration framework.

4. **New Zealand: Relative Portrayal and Agreement Legislative issues**

New Zealand's model for settling political gridlock spins around corresponding portrayal and agreement legislative issues. The country's constituent framework, in view of relative portrayal, guarantees that ideological groups get seats with respect to their portion of the vote. This framework cultivates a multiparty political scene, empowering coordinated effort and agreement building.

New Zealand's progress in defeating political gridlock is exemplified by its treatment of the electing framework change during the 1990s.

The reception of a blended part relative (MMP) discretionary framework was a critical shift that meant to address the constraints of the past first-past-the-post framework. The MMP framework supports the arrangement of alliance state run administrations and requires cross-party collaboration, limiting the gamble of authoritative halt.

The accentuation on agreement governmental issues in New Zealand guarantees that key choices mirror an expansive understanding among ideological groups. Pioneers take part in exchange and split the difference, looking for shared view to resolve major problems. The outcome of New Zealand's corresponding portrayal framework lies in its capacity to oblige assorted political viewpoints, encouraging successful administration.

5. **South Africa: Compromise and Country Building**

South Africa's model for settling political gridlock is established in the standards of compromise and country building. The nation's progress from politically-sanctioned racial segregation to a vote based system included a significant obligation to tending to verifiable treacheries and encouraging social union. Reality and Compromise Commission (TRC) assumed a focal part in this groundbreaking system.

The TRC, led by Diocese supervisor Desmond Tutu, gave a stage to casualties and culprits of politically-sanctioned racial segregation period outrages to share their accounts. The commission meant to reveal reality, advance responsibility, and add to the recuperating of a profoundly isolated society. The accentuation on compromise turned into a core value in the post-politically sanctioned racial segregation time, making way for a cooperative way to deal with administration.

South Africa's outcome in beating political gridlock is apparent in its obligation to inclusivity and tending to verifiable disparities. The public authority's strategies, for example, governmental policy regarding minorities in society and land change, mirror a devotion to building an all the more and fair society. By focusing on compromise and country building, South Africa epitomizes a model for beating the difficulties of administration established in verifiable divisions.

6. **Norway: Social Discourse and Agreement Based Direction**

Norway's model for settling political gridlock puts serious areas of strength for an on friendly discourse and agreement based independent direction. The country's obligation to a social market economy, joined with a powerful government assistance state, mirrors an administration model that focuses on coordinated effort among government, businesses, and worker's guilds.

The Norwegian social discourse model includes customary conferences and dealings between the public authority, businesses, and worker's organizations. This cooperative methodology guarantees that key arrangement choices, especially those connected with work and monetary issues, are made with input from all partners. The emphasis on agreement based independent direction limits the gamble of political gridlock emerging from clashing interests.

Norway's outcome in beating gridlock is clear in its capacity to offset monetary seriousness with social government assistance. The obligation to social exchange has added to a stable political and financial climate, encouraging viable administration. The Norwegian model offers bits of knowledge into the groundbreaking capability of cooperative dynamic in tending to complex cultural difficulties.

7. **Costa Rica: Demilitarization and Tranquil Administration**

Costa Rica's model for settling political gridlock focuses on demobilization and a guarantee to quiet administration. The country, with a long history of political soundness and the shortfall of a standing armed force starting around 1949, represents a novel way to deal with tending to security challenges through conciliatory means.

The choice to disband the military in Costa Rica was a strong move that flagged a promise to quiet conjunction and the goal of contentions through discourse. By redistributing assets from the military to social projects, Costa Rica focused on interests in training, medical care, and ecological preservation. This model has added to a culture of quiet administration and limited the gamble of political gridlock emerging from militarization.

Costa Rica's progress in conquering gridlock is attached to its commitment to neutralization and the quest for political answers for clashes. The shortfall of a standing armed force cultivates a world of politics zeroed in on tending to cultural necessities and building a strong and feasible society. The Costa Rican model offers a convincing illustration of how demobilization can add to successful administration.

Incorporating Examples for Groundbreaking Initiative

The assessment of fruitful models for settling political gridlock across different nations uncovers an embroidery of techniques and approaches that pioneers can draw upon for groundbreaking initiative. From the alliance agreement model in Germany to the demobilization model in Costa Rica, each contextual analysis gives significant experiences into the multi-layered nature of viable administration.

The consistent ideas woven through these models incorporate a promise to coordinated effort, inclusivity, down to earth navigation, and an emphasis on tending to verifiable treacheries. Pioneers who effectively explored through political difficulties embraced the standards of compromise, agreement building, and social attachment. The capacity to focus on the benefit of all over momentary political additions arose as a focal subject in extraordinary administration.

As countries wrestle with the intricacies of political gridlock, the examples gathered from fruitful models offer an outline for pioneers looking to get through ensnarements and encourage successful, principled administration. The incorporation of these examples, customized to the remarkable settings of every country, turns into a groundbreaking power fit for controlling social orders toward flexibility, solidarity, and feasible advancement.

5.3 Lessons that can be learned from international experiences in addressing political challenges.

Examples Gained from Worldwide Encounters in Tending to Political Difficulties: A Worldwide Point of view

As the world explores a period of extraordinary political intricacies, drawing illustrations from global encounters becomes fundamental in tending to political difficulties. This section investigates a different cluster of worldwide points of view, looking at contextual investigations from different nations to distil important examples for pioneers trying to encourage compelling administration, explore political traps, and advance versatility despite difficulty.

1. **Germany: Agreement Working in Alliance Administration**

    Germany's political scene, portrayed by multiparty frameworks and alliance legislatures, offers a convincing example in agreement building. The capacity to explore political variety and encourage cooperation among alliance accomplices has been instrumental in conquering gridlock and progressing compelling administration. German pioneers, especially Chancellor Angela Merkel, have exhibited that a guarantee to agreement building and compromise can prompt stable administration even amidst complex difficulties.

    The example from Germany highlights the significance of political pioneers developing a feeling of coordinated effort, embracing different viewpoints, and focusing on the benefit of all over sectarian interests. In alliance administration, the craft of exchange turns into a key part in getting through political impasses, featuring the groundbreaking capability of agreement based direction.

2. **South Africa: Compromise as a Way to Mending**

The South African experience, set apart by the change from politically-sanctioned racial segregation to a majority rules government, gives a significant example in the force of compromise. The foundation of Reality and Compromise Commission (TRC) under the initiative of Ecclesiastical overseer Desmond Tutu represents a pledge to tending to verifiable treacheries through discourse, affirmation, and mending.

The South African example underlines the groundbreaking effect of pioneers who focus on compromise over retaliation. By making a stage for casualties and culprits to share their accounts, South Africa cultivated a public exchange that pointed toward building a more comprehensive and just society. The accentuation on compromise turns into a useful asset for pioneers trying to defeat well established verifiable divisions and join social orders cracked by political hardship.

3. **Singapore: Technocratic Administration and Long haul Vision**

Singapore's model of technocratic administration, exemplified by its initial architect Lee Kuan Yew, gives an illustration in the significance of long haul vision and vital preparation. Lee Kuan Yew's obligation to meritocracy, even minded administration, and an emphasis on technocratic skill assumed a vital part in changing Singapore into a monetary force to be reckoned with.

The Singaporean illustration features the meaning of pioneers who focus on aptitude, proof based navigation, and long haul arranging. By cultivating a culture of meritocracy and depending on the mastery of experts, Singapore shows the way that technocratic initiative can add to powerful administration and practical turn of events.

4. **Norway: Social Discourse and Comprehensive Navigation**

Norway's outcome in addressing political provokes is grounded in its obligation to social discourse and comprehensive direction. The Norwegian model, described by standard discussions and talks between the public authority, businesses, and worker's guilds, epitomizes the force of cooperative ways to deal with administration.

The Norwegian illustration highlights the groundbreaking capability of pioneers who effectively take part in friendly exchange, looking for input from different partners. By guaranteeing that choices are made with thought for different points of view, Norway exhibits the versatility of an administration model based on inclusivity, participation, and a promise to adjusting financial and social needs.

5. **Canada: Multiculturalism and Comprehensive Administration**

Canada's way to deal with multiculturalism and comprehensive administration gives a significant example to pioneers exploring different social orders. The accentuation on embracing and celebrating social variety, as well as tending to verifiable treacheries, has gained notoriety for comprehensive administration. The Canadian illustration highlights the significance of pioneers who champion variety, value, and consideration as central standards of administration. By recognizing and correcting verifiable wrongs, as found in drives like Reality and Compromise Commission, Canada exhibits how embracing multiculturalism can encourage a stronger and joined society.

6. **Costa Rica: Demobilization and Quest for Serene Administration**

Costa Rica's choice to disband its military and seek after quiet administration offers a one of a kind example in tending to political difficulties through disarmament. By redistributing assets from the military to social projects, Costa Rica focuses on interests in training, medical services, and natural protection. The Costa Rican example features the extraordinary capability of pioneers who focus on tranquil arrangements over militarization. By encouraging a culture of strategy and compromise, Costa Rica gives a model to countries trying to beat political difficulties without depending on furnished struggle.

7. **New Zealand: Relative Portrayal and Versatility**

New Zealand's reception of corresponding portrayal and its ensuing electing framework change offer an example in political flexibility. The shift to a blended part relative (MMP) discretionary framework mirrors a guarantee to tending to the restrictions of the past first-past-the-post framework and supports coordinated effort in administration.

The New Zealand illustration underscores the significance of pioneers who will adjust and change political frameworks to more readily line up with cultural requirements. By embracing corresponding portrayal, New Zealand grandstands how political flexibility can add to more responsive and powerful administration.

8. **Brazil: Tending to Defilement for Successful Administration**

Brazil's involvement with tending to defilement through components like denunciation procedures offers an example in the significance of responsibility for viable administration. The prosecution of Brazilian presidents, for example, Dilma Rousseff and Michel Temer, highlights the groundbreaking effect of pioneers who focus on responsibility and straightforwardness.

The Brazilian example features the basic of pioneers who will face debasement inside political organizations. By considering pioneers responsible for bad behavior, Brazil embodies how addressing debasement can add to reestablishing public trust and encouraging more successful administration.

Incorporating Worldwide Examples for Extraordinary Administration

The illustrations gained from worldwide encounters in tending to political difficulties structure a rich embroidery of experiences for pioneers exploring the intricacies of administration. From agreement working in Germany to compromise in South Africa, and from technocratic administration in Singapore to comprehensive administration in Canada, each contextual analysis offers one of a kind viewpoints on powerful administration.

Incorporating these worldwide illustrations uncovers ongoing ideas that wind through effective ways to deal with administration. The extraordinary capability of pioneers who focus on joint effort, compromise, technocratic mastery, social discourse, multiculturalism, demobilization, versatility, and responsibility arises as a focal topic.

As pioneers defy political difficulties in an interconnected world, the combination of these illustrations turns into an aide for groundbreaking initiative. By drawing on the aggregate insight acquired from different worldwide encounters, pioneers can explore political intricacies, cultivate strength in their social orders, and add to the progression of successful and principled administration on a worldwide scale.

Chapter 6

Mobilizing for Change

Activating for Change: Techniques, Difficulties, and Wins

In the consistently developing scene of worldwide administration, preparing for change remains as a considerable errand, requiring vital vision, grassroots commitment, and a promise to extraordinary authority. This section investigates the diverse components of activation for change, digging into contextual analyses, methodologies, difficulties, and wins that have described developments pointed toward reshaping political scenes, propelling civil rights, and encouraging positive cultural changes.

1. **The Force of Grassroots Developments: Illustrations from Social liberties**

   The archives of history are loaded with cases where grassroots developments have been impetuses for change. The Social liberties Development in the US during the mid-twentieth century fills in as a paradigmatic model. Driven by the mission for racial uniformity and equity, grassroots activists, drove by notorious figures like Martin Luther Ruler Jr., assembled millions to request a finish to isolation, biased rehearses, and fundamental bigotry.

   The example from the Social equality Development lies in the strength of grassroots assembly to excite aggregate activity and push for extraordinary change. From the Montgomery Transport Blacklist to the Walk on Washington, these developments outfit the force of peaceful obstruction, common defiance, and vital assembly to challenge instilled frameworks of abuse. The outcome of the Social liberties Development outlines the persevering through effect of grassroots drives in affecting cultural changes.

2. **Computerized Activism and the Middle Easterner Spring: The Job of Innovation in Activation**

The appearance of the computerized age has introduced new roads for activation, as found in the Bedouin Spring uprisings that cleared across the Center East and North Africa in 2010-2011. Empowered by web-based entertainment stages, computerized activism turned into a powerful power for putting together fights, scattering data, and preparing populaces against despotic systems. From Tunisia to Egypt, the Bedouin Spring showed the groundbreaking capability of innovation in enhancing voices, cultivating network, and assembling for change.

The example from the Bedouin Spring lies in the double edged nature of advanced activism. While innovation works with quick preparation and the dispersal of data, it likewise presents difficulties like government observation, control of stories, and the potential for virtual entertainment to turn into an instrument for spreading deception. The Middle Easterner Spring highlights the significance of tackling advanced apparatuses wisely and grasping their constraints chasing significant change.

3. **Environment Activism and Worldwide Activation: Greta Thunberg and Fridays for Future**

The desperation of tending to environmental change has catalyzed another rush of worldwide activation, with youth activists at the very front. Greta Thunberg, a Swedish teen, arose as an image of environment activism through her Fridays for Future development. Which began as a singular school strike for environment activity blossomed into a worldwide peculiarity, preparing a large number of youngsters overall to request unequivocal activity against environmental change.

The illustration from environment activism lies in the power of grassroots developments drove by enthusiastic people. Greta Thunberg's capacity to prepare a worldwide youth development highlights the effect of restricted activities reverberating on a planetary scale. The interconnectedness of ecological issues and the force of grassroots activation to rise above borders feature the groundbreaking capability of aggregate activity notwithstanding existential dangers.

4. **Ladies' Developments and the Battle for Uniformity: #MeToo and Then some**

Ladies' developments have generally assumed a significant part in testing orientation imbalance and pushing for ladies' privileges. The #MeToo development, which picked up speed in 2017, embodies the force of social assembly in resolving foundational issues of lewd behavior and attack. Starting from grassroots activism, #MeToo provoked a worldwide discussion, rising above enterprises, boundaries, and progressive systems.

The illustration from the #MeToo development lies in the capacity of grassroots drives to start social moves and request responsibility. By utilizing virtual entertainment stages, overcomers of sexual wrongdoing shared their accounts, cultivating fortitude and testing settled in power structures. The development highlighted the meaning of intensifying minimized voices, assembling public help, and inducing fundamental changes to resolve inescapable issues of orientation based savagery.

5. **Native Privileges and Land Developments: Standing Stone and Then some**

The battle for native freedoms and ecological equity has been exemplified by developments, for example, the Standing Stone fights against the Dakota Access Pipeline. Local American people group, joined by activists and partners, activated to safeguard consecrated lands, water assets, and the privileges of native people groups. The Standing Stone fights turned into a point of convergence for worldwide native privileges developments, exciting help and revealing insight into issues of land sway.

The illustration from native privileges developments is the significance of assembling around issues profoundly associated with social personality and natural stewardship. The Standing Stone fights highlighted the strength of networks guarding their familial terrains and the need of enhancing native voices chasing equity. Preparing for native freedoms fills in as a demonstration of the getting through strength of developments grounded in social protection and natural manageability.

6. **Hong Kong's Favorable to A majority rules system Development: Exploring Constraint**

The favorable to a vote based system development in Hong Kong, especially the fights that unfurled in 2019, gives experiences into the difficulties of preparing for change in a climate set apart by political constraint. Residents of Hong Kong, essentially youth activists, activated against apparent infringements on their independence by central area China. The fights, set apart by inventive strategies and inescapable preparation, tried to protect popularity based standards and safeguard the interesting personality of Hong Kong.

The illustration from Hong Kong's favorable to a majority rules government development lies in the versatility of activists exploring severe circumstances. Confronting police ruthlessness, captures, and the inconvenience of public safety regulations, protestors adjusted their systems while utilizing worldwide help. The development highlights the difficulties of preparing under tyrant systems and features the significance of worldwide fortitude despite restraint.

7. **People of color Matter: From Neighborhood Activism to Worldwide Development**

The People of color Matter (BLM) development, touched off by the killing of Trayvon Martin in 2012 and acquiring conspicuousness after the passings of Michael Brown, Eric Collect, and George Floyd, represents the groundbreaking effect of preparation against fundamental bigotry and police mercilessness. Starting as a neighborhood reaction to racial foul play, BLM expanded into a worldwide development, preparing millions to request a finish to fundamental prejudice and supporter for police change.

The illustration from the People of color Matter development lies in the capacity to make an interpretation of restricted complaints into a worldwide call for equity. Grassroots coordinators, using web-based entertainment and direct activity, pushed the development onto the global stage, cultivating discussions about racial disparity, policing, and fundamental unfairness. BLM highlights the extraordinary force of preparing against profoundly settled in designs of separation.

8. **Difficulties and Wins of Preparation**

Preparing for change isn't without its difficulties. Activists frequently face obstruction from dug in power structures, risk brutality and suppression, and wrestle with interior divisions. The test lies in supporting force, encouraging inclusivity, and exploring the intricacies of diversity. In any case, wins proliferate when developments effectively impact strategy changes, shift social accounts, and flash enduring cultural changes.

Wins in preparation are apparent in strategy changes catalyzed by developments, social movements testing cultural standards, and the strengthening of underestimated networks. The victory of the LGBTQ+ privileges development, for instance, has prompted legitimate acknowledgment, social acknowledgment, and strategy changes across the globe. The accomplishments of preparation highlight the getting through effect of aggregate activity in reshaping the direction of social orders.

Preparing for an Aggregate Future

Preparing for change stays a dynamic and fundamental undertaking in the journey for an all the more, fair, and manageable world. The examples drawn from grassroots developments, computerized activism, environment activity, ladies' privileges, native battles, supportive of a vote based system developments, hostile to bigoted drives, and the victories and difficulties they include, by and large add to the advancing story of groundbreaking initiative.

As social orders wrestle with major problems going from environment emergencies to foundational imbalances, the preparation for change turns into a basic for aggregate advancement. The combination of these illustrations highlights the general standards of enhancing minimized voices, cultivating inclusivity, utilizing innovation wisely, and exploring difficulties with flexibility. In the interconnected embroidery of worldwide developments, the call to prepare for an aggregate future resounds as a persevering through force for positive change.

6.1 Exploration of grassroots movements and citizen initiatives that have successfully challenged political stalemate.

Investigation of Grassroots Developments and Resident Drives: Impetuses for Testing Political Impasse

In the domain of administration, where political impasses frequently hinder progress, grassroots developments and resident drives arise as strong impetuses for change. This section dives into a far reaching investigation of occasions where normal residents, energized by energy and a guarantee to cultural prosperity, have effectively tested political impasses. From pushing for strategy changes to molding the talk, these grassroots developments exhibit the extraordinary capability of aggregate activity in exploring and conquering settled in political gridlock.

1. **Possess Money Road: Revealing Monetary Imbalances**

   The Possess Money Road development that picked up speed in 2011 stands as a demonstration of the capacity of grassroots drives to challenge political and monetary impasses. Started by the discontent over financial imbalances, corporate impact, and the apparent disappointment of political foundations to resolve these issues, nonconformists consumed public spaces, especially Zuccotti Park in New York City.

   The Possess development turned into an image of aggregate dissatisfaction with business as usual, stressing the effect of financial inconsistencies on cultural prosperity. By laying out settlements and arranging fights, members looked to cause to notice the lopsided impact of monetary organizations in policymaking. However deficient with regards to a unified administration structure, the development prevailed with regards to moving public talk, provoking conversations about pay imbalance, corporate responsibility, and the job of cash in legislative issues.

   The illustration from Possess Money Road lies in the limit of grassroots developments to push issues onto the public plan, even without any particular approach requests. By encouraging a feeling of shared complaint and preparing residents across different foundations, the development tested political impasses by reevaluating the story around financial equity and disparity.

2. **Mothers Request Activity: Pushing for Weapon Control**

   Despite political dormancy encompassing weapon control regulation in the US, Mothers Request Activity for Firearm Sense in America arose as a strong grassroots development. Established in the repercussions of the Sandy Snare Grade School shooting in 2012, this development contains moms and concerned residents upholding for presence of mind firearm wellbeing measures.

   Mothers Request Activity exhibits how resident drives, frequently drove by those straightforwardly impacted by an issue, can challenge dug in political positions. By utilizing the close to home load of parental concern and sorting out through neighborhood sections, the development has effectively impacted strategy changes at both state and government levels. Its methodology underscores building associations with legislators, utilizing grassroots campaigning, and countering the impact of strong vested parties.

The illustration from Mothers Request Activity lies in the viability of grassroots developments that attention on unambiguous strategy goals and take part in essential promotion. By adapting the issue and enhancing the voices of those straightforwardly affected, the development has added to breaking political impasses and propelling discussions around firearm control.

3. **The Umbrella Development in Hong Kong: Requesting Vote based Changes**

The Umbrella Development that unfurled in Hong Kong in 2014 was a supportive of a majority rules system development that carried large number of residents to the roads to request political changes. Confronted with political stagnation and restricted progress toward widespread testimonial, especially in the appointment of the CEO, residents, essentially drove by youthful activists, took part in common rebellion and involved key region of the city.

The Umbrella Development shows the strength of grassroots developments in testing political impasses, even despite huge resistance from specialists. By taking on imaginative types of peaceful dissent, including the utilization of umbrellas to safeguard against poisonous gas, members accumulated worldwide consideration and attracted concentration to the requirement for certified popularity based changes.

The illustration from the Umbrella Development lies in the assurance of residents to challenge political latency and request a say in their administration. Grassroots developments, driven by a pledge to popularity based standards, can act as strong instruments in testing political impasses and squeezing for significant changes.

4. **Indissoluble: Grassroots Protection from Trump Organization Approaches**

In the consequence of the 2016 U.S. official political race, Unified arose as a grassroots development zeroed in on opposing the strategies of the Trump organization. Established by previous legislative staff members, the development gave a manual to residents to connect with their chosen delegates really, drawing motivation from the Casual get-together's progress in impacting political talk.

Unbreakable epitomizes how common residents can coordinate locally to challenge political impasses on a public scale. By applying tension through official Q&A events, calls, and composed backing endeavors, the development tried to consider administrators responsible and oppose arrangements saw as destructive to majority rule standards and common liberties.

The illustration from Unbreakable lies in the essential utilization of grassroots getting sorted out to challenge political standards and oppose arrangements saw as negative. The development shows that resident drives, outfitted with a reasonable system and an emphasis on restricted activism, can act as an imposing power in molding the political scene.

5. **Yellow Vest Development in France: Directing Famous Discontent**

The Yellow Vest development that emitted in France in 2018 addressed a decentralized grassroots uprising against financial disparity, high living expenses, and saw government lack of concern. Starting from a request against fuel charge climbs, the development quickly developed into a more extensive articulation of discontent, including fights, street bars, and conflicts with specialists.

The Yellow Vest development features how apparently limited complaints can combine into a cross country articulation of disappointment, testing political stagnation. Regardless of lacking proper administration, the development constrained President Emmanuel Macron to make concessions, including pulling out the fuel charge increment and reporting measures to address financial incongruities.

The example from the Yellow Vest development lies in the capability of grassroots drives to channel well known discontent and challenge political detachment. By taking advantage of broad disappointment and putting together decentralized fights, residents can impact political talk and push for strategy changes.

6. **GetUp!: Promotion for Moderate Approaches in Australia**

GetUp!, established in 2005, is an Australian grassroots development that backers for moderate approaches and considers political pioneers responsible. Working as a free association, GetUp! uses computerized stages and local area coordinating to prepare residents around issues, for example, environmental change, civil rights, and vote based changes.

GetUp! epitomizes the versatility of grassroots developments in using computerized apparatuses to challenge political impasses. By utilizing on the web stages for raising support, promotion, and preparation, the development has turned into a strong power in molding popular assessment and impacting strategy banters in Australia.

The illustration from GetUp! lies in the essential utilization of innovation and local area coordinating to challenge political idleness. Grassroots developments, by embracing computerized instruments and taking on a diverse methodology, can really connect with residents and impact political results.

7. **Fridays for Future: Youth-Drove Environment Activism**

Fridays for Future, started by Greta Thunberg in 2018, has quickly developed into a worldwide youth-drove development pushing for critical environment activity.

Beginning as a lone school strike for environment outside the Swedish parliament, the development has since motivated great many understudies overall to partake in strikes, fights, and promotion endeavors.

Fridays for Future features the groundbreaking capability of youth-drove grassroots developments in testing political lack of concern on a worldwide scale. By enhancing the voices of youthful activists, the development has prevailed with regards to putting environmental change high on the worldwide plan and requesting unequivocal activity from political pioneers.

The example from Fridays for Future lies in the power of grassroots developments drove by the more youthful age. By preparing understudies, utilizing web-based entertainment, and partaking in composed worldwide strikes, the development challenges political idleness and requests responsibility on one of the most major problems within recent memory.

The Strength of Grassroots Developments

The investigation of grassroots developments and resident drives uncovers a consistent idea of strength and extraordinary potential. Whether testing monetary variations, supporting for strategy changes, or requesting popularity based changes, these developments grandstand the getting through force of aggregate activity in exploring and conquering political impasses.

The illustrations drawn from Possess Money Road, Mothers Request Activity, the Umbrella Development, Unbreakable, the Yellow Vest development, GetUp!, and Fridays for Future highlight the significance of confined activism, vital backing, and utilizing innovation. Grassroots developments, driven by a pledge to cultural prosperity, basic freedoms, and majority rule standards, can act as impressive influencers, testing political idleness and reshaping the direction of administration.

As residents keep on going up against political difficulties, the accounts of these grassroots developments stand as signals of motivation and demonstration of the persevering through effect of aggregate activity. In this present reality where political impasses continue, the flexibility of grassroots drives stays a strong power, equipped for directing social orders towards more comprehensive, just, and responsive administration.

6.2 Analysis of the role of civil society in pressuring political leaders to act.

Examination of the Job of Common Society in Constraining Political Pioneers to Act: Impetuses for Change

Common society, containing people and associations outside the public authority and business circles, assumes an essential part in molding political scenes and considering pioneers responsible. This examination digs into the complex elements of common society's part in compelling political pioneers to act. From grassroots activism to backing associations, common society goes about as a basic impetus for change, pushing political pioneers to resolve major problems, maintain common freedoms, and cultivate responsive administration.

1. **Grassroots Activism: Enhancing Voices From the beginning**

   At the core of common society's impact is grassroots activism, where people at the nearby level activate to address local area concerns. These grassroots developments frequently arise as a reaction to neglected requirements, treachery, or natural difficulties. For example, in the battle against racial disparity, developments like People of color Matter have activated residents at the grassroots level to request political activity.

   Grassroots activism brings a direct, unfiltered voice from individuals to political pioneers. By coordinating fights, participating in common defiance, and utilizing web-based entertainment, grassroots developments can collect broad consideration and make a groundswell of public help. The force of these developments lies in their capacity to challenge political pioneers by introducing an aggregate and energetic interest for change.

2. **Backing Associations: Exploring Strategy Discussions**

   Common society is home to a plenty of support associations that work at neighborhood, public, and global levels. These associations act as master voices, leading examination, forming popular assessment, and taking part in arrangement discusses. They go about as middle people between general society and political pioneers, making an interpretation of resident worries into noteworthy strategy proposals.

   Common liberties associations, natural gatherings, and research organizations embody the variety of backing associations inside common society. Reprieve Worldwide, for example, champions worldwide common freedoms causes, coming down on political pioneers to resolve issues like torment, separation, and detainment of activists. Through reports, crusades, and legitimate backing, these associations shape the story around basic issues and consider pioneers responsible for their activities.

3. **Guard dog Job: Viewing Ability to be answerable**

   One of the major jobs of common society is going about as a guard dog, investigating the activities of political pioneers and establishments. This investigation is fundamental for keeping up with straightforwardness, responsibility, and law and order. Non-legislative associations (NGOs), analytical writers, and resident drove drives frequently assume this basic part.

   For example, associations like Straightforwardness Worldwide spotlight on battling defilement by uncovering degenerate practices and upholding for foundational changes. By observing government activities, these guard dogs act as a keep an eye on the maltreatment of force and guarantee that political pioneers are liable to the general population. The guard dog job stretches out to advancing moral direct, forestalling maltreatments of power, and shielding popularity based standards.

4. **Alliance Building: Strength in Numbers**

   Common society succeeds in uniting assorted voices through alliance building. Perceiving that aggregate strength is many times more significant, backing bunches unite to address shared concerns. Alliances can prepare a more extensive base, making a brought together front that is more hard for political pioneers to disregard.

   The Ladies' Walk, an alliance of different ladies' privileges gatherings, embodies the force of aggregate activity. By joining under a typical pennant, these associations enhance their effect, causing to notice issues like orientation fairness, conceptive freedoms, and savagery against ladies. Alliance building improves the limit of common society to apply tension on political pioneers, making it harder for them to excuse the requests of a unified front.

5. **Metro Commitment: Spanning Holes in Portrayal**

   Common society goes about as a scaffold among residents and political pioneers, encouraging city commitment and support. In many cases, underestimated gatherings or networks get comfortable with themselves enhanced through common society associations that champion their causes. By tending to holes in portrayal, common society guarantees that the worries of all residents are brought to the very front.

   Local area based associations, backing bunches for minorities, and stages elevating urban schooling add to the inclusivity of city commitment. These associations enable people to partake in political cycles, from neighborhood decision-production to public races. The more drawn in residents are, the more political pioneers are constrained to think about the assorted requirements and viewpoints of their constituents.

6. **Worldwide Backing: Worldwide Strain for Neighborhood Change**

   Common society works on a worldwide scale, utilizing worldwide organizations to resolve neighborhood issues. Worldwide NGOs, for example, Basic liberties Watch or Greenpeace, use transnational support to constrain political pioneers to institute change. By speaking to worldwide standards, common liberties principles, and ecological obligations, common society associations make a snare of strain that rises above public limits.

   The worldwide environment strikes drove by associations like Fridays for Future exhibit the internationalization of common society developments. Propelled by Greta Thunberg, youth activists all over the planet participated in composed fights, requesting atrocity on environmental change. The global fortitude made by common society drives amplifies the tension on political pioneers, underlining that specific issues can't be secluded inside public lines.

7. **Lawful Support: Authorizing Responsibility Through Courts**

   Common society associations frequently resort to legitimate support to uphold responsibility and challenge political pioneers through legal means.

Whether it's basic freedoms infringement, natural debasement, or breaks of established standards, lawful activity fills in as a strong device in the common society munititions stockpile.

Associations like the American Common Freedoms Association (ACLU) in the US or the Middle for Strategy Options in Sri Lanka represent the effect of lawful promotion. By indicting cases, these associations challenge unlawful arrangements, request straightforwardness, and look for equity for minimized gatherings. The legitimate pathway gives an organized system to common society to consider political pioneers responsible inside the structure of law and order.

8. **City Innovation: Improving Resident Support**

In the computerized age, city innovation, or "city tech," has arisen as an integral asset inside common society to upgrade resident support and consider political pioneers responsible. Online stages, applications, and computerized devices engage residents to connect straightforwardly in administration processes, screen government exercises, and take part in direction.

Stages like FixMyStreet, which permits residents to report nearby issues to specialists, or drives like MySociety, which advances city tech for straightforwardness, grandstand the capability of innovation to overcome any barrier among residents and political pioneers. Urban tech drives add to the decentralization of force, making political pioneers more receptive to the ongoing requirements and worries of their constituents.

The Elements of Impact

In the mind boggling dance between common society and political pioneers, the elements of impact are molded by a scope of variables.

Grassroots activism brings crude, unfiltered requests starting from the earliest stage, promotion associations explore strategy discusses and contribute aptitude. The guard dog job guarantees responsibility, alliance developing makes fortitude in solidarity, and municipal commitment spans holes in portrayal.

Worldwide support expands tension across borders, lawful promotion authorizes responsibility through courts, and metro innovation changes resident cooperation in administration. Together, these features structure a mind boggling environment where common society goes about as both a keep an eye on power and an impetus for change. The capacity of common society to constrain political pioneers to act lies in its flexibility, inclusivity, and obligation to the standards of equity, straightforwardness, and basic freedoms.

As political pioneers explore the requests and assumptions for their constituents, common society stays a strong power, constantly developing to address the difficulties of a unique political scene. The persevering through impact of common society highlights its fundamental job in forming responsive, responsible, and comprehensive administration. In the continuous mission for an all the more and fair world, the joint effort between common society and political pioneers stays essential, characterizing the shapes of popularity based social orders and guaranteeing the satisfaction of the common agreement among residents and their chiefs.

6.3 Strategies for mobilizing public support and fostering civic engagement to break the deadlock.

Systems for Preparing Public Help and Encouraging Metro Commitment: A Plan for Breaking the Gridlock

Notwithstanding political impasse and gridlock, preparing public help and cultivating city commitment arises as a significant procedure for breaking the stalemate. This section investigates an extensive diagram enveloping different procedures pointed toward stimulating residents, enhancing their voices, and developing dynamic support in the vote based process. From grassroots developments to computerized advancements, the accompanying techniques structure a complex way to deal with exploring political halts and reviving municipal commitment.

1. **Grassroots Activation: Enabling People group From the beginning**

   At the center of breaking political stop is the force of grassroots preparation. Networks have one of a kind experiences into their requirements, and by engaging them, political pioneers can take advantage of a wellspring of thoughts and energy. Drives like municipal events, local area discussions, and participatory dynamic cycles give stages to residents to straightforwardly voice their interests.

   Drawing in with neighborhood networks encourages a feeling of pride and organization, separating the impression of separation among residents and political cycles. Pioneers who effectively stand by listening to grassroots developments exhibit a promise to responsive administration, flagging a takeoff from dug in places. Whether through area soliciting or local area studios, grassroots assembly lays the basis for reviving metro commitment.

2. **Advanced Stages and Virtual Entertainment: Enhancing Voices in the Computerized Age**

   In a period overwhelmed by innovation, computerized stages and web-based entertainment act as useful assets for preparing public help. Drawing in residents through web-based stages works with continuous correspondence as well as empowers the quick spread of data. Web-based entertainment crusades, hashtags, and computerized petitions can transform individual voices into an aggregate thunder, rising above geographic hindrances.

   The Middle Easterner Spring, for instance, delineated the extraordinary capability of computerized stages in assembling masses for political change. Pioneers trying to break a stop can use these devices to construct online networks, share strategy proposition, and rally public help. Nonetheless, an essential methodology is fundamental, as computerized commitment requires validness, responsiveness, and versatility to reverberate with different crowds really.

3. **Comprehensive Direction: Building Scaffolds Across Different Viewpoints**

   Political halts frequently emerge from firmly established divisions and philosophical contrasts. Pioneers can break the stalemate by embracing comprehensive dynamic cycles that unite different points of view. Laying out resident gatherings, warning sheets, or comprehensive teams guarantees that a wide range of voices is viewed as in strategy detailing.

   This approach encourages municipal commitment as well as upgrades the authenticity of choices, as residents see their contribution as essential to the cycle. Pioneers who effectively look for input from different segment gatherings, including underestimated networks, exhibit a promise to addressing the sum of their supporters. Comprehensive direction turns into an impetus for breaking political gridlocks by rising above hardliner partitions and cultivating a feeling of shared proprietorship.

4. **Public-Private Associations: Utilizing Aggregate Assets for Change**

   Breaking a political halt frequently requires inventive arrangements that go past the extent of government assets alone. Public-private organizations (PPPs) offer an essential road for pioneers to prepare extra assets, skill, and viewpoints from the confidential area. Joint efforts with organizations, nonbenefits, and local area associations can infuse groundbreaking thoughts and energy into strategy drives.

   By encouraging organizations with different partners, pioneers show a pledge to cooperative administration, creating some distance from the thought of political disconnection. PPPs can address complex difficulties, for example, framework improvement or social government assistance programs, with an all encompassing methodology that use the qualities of both public and confidential areas. This procedure separates storehouses as well as encourages a feeling of divided liability between residents.

5. **Local area Based Drives: Putting resources into Neighborhood Arrangements**

   Enabling people group to assume responsibility for their fates is a strong system for breaking political halt. Pioneers can put resources into local area based drives that address explicit nearby difficulties and encourage a healthy identity viability among residents. This could incorporate supporting neighborhood business people, empowering local area drove advancement ventures, or financing grassroots associations that hero social causes.

   At the point when residents witness substantial upgrades coming about because of neighborhood drives, they become more put resources into the political interaction. This system not just breaks the halt at the nearby level yet additionally adds to a more extensive story of local area driven change. By perceiving and supporting local area flexibility, pioneers can revitalize metro commitment and rouse residents to take part in forming their future effectively.

6. **Training and Metro Proficiency: Enabling Informed Residents**

Breaking political stop requires an educated and connected with populace. Pioneers can put resources into training and municipal proficiency programs that furnish residents with the information and abilities to take part in the popularity based process effectively. Municipal training, whether in schools or through local area studios, enables people to grasp the intricacies of administration, basically break down arrangements, and participate in informed discusses.

Pioneers who focus on municipal proficiency exhibit a guarantee to straightforwardness and responsibility. Informed residents are bound to effectively take part in races, advocate for their inclinations, and consider pioneers responsible for their activities. By putting resources into schooling, pioneers lay the preparation for breaking the gridlock by developing a populace that isn't just educated yet in addition effectively engaged with molding the political scene.

7. **Public Mindfulness Missions: Imparting a Dream for Change**

Openness is absolutely vital in assembling public help and breaking political gridlock. Pioneers should explain a convincing vision for change, really convey strategy recommendations, and take part in straightforward and open discourse with the general population. Public mindfulness crusades, whether through conventional media, web-based entertainment, or local area occasions, assume a vital part in molding public discernment.

Compelling correspondence includes passing data as well as effectively tuning in on to resident worries. Pioneers who participate in two-manner correspondence, recognizing public criticism and adjusting approaches appropriately, assemble trust and validity. Public mindfulness crusades act as a vehicle for pioneers to interface with residents, cultivate understanding, and rally support for drives pointed toward breaking the political stop.

8. **Responsive Administration: Tending to Prompt Worries**

To assemble public help and break political halt, pioneers should exhibit responsiveness to quick worries. This includes quick activity on issues that straightforwardly influence residents' lives. Whether it's tending to financial difficulties, medical care difficulties, or ecological issues, pioneers who answer proactively to squeezing concerns fabricate trust and validity.

A responsive administration approach includes consistent input circles, customary official Q&A events, and components for residents to voice their interests. By tending to prompt difficulties, pioneers make a groundwork of public help that can be utilized to handle more complicated, long haul issues adding to political gridlock.

An All encompassing Way to deal with Recharged Urban Commitment

Breaking political stop requires an all encompassing and diverse methodology that tends to the underlying drivers of stagnation while effectively captivating residents in the majority rule process. From grassroots preparation to comprehensive direction, public-private organizations, and schooling drives, the procedures illustrated in this outline offer pioneers a complete manual for revitalizing municipal commitment and assembling public help.

The interconnected idea of these systems stresses the requirement for pioneers to embrace a nuanced and versatile methodology. A mix of on the web and disconnected commitment, comprehensive navigation, and responsive administration can make a dynamic and participatory political scene. In breaking the gridlock, pioneers open the potential for strategy development as well as encourage a reestablished feeling of community obligation and obligation among residents, eventually reinforcing the underpinnings of a majority rules system.

Chapter 7

Charting a Path Forward

Diagramming a Way ahead: Exploring the Perplexing Territory of Political Impasse and Recharging Majority rule Imperativeness

In the maze of political impasse, where dug in places and fundamental difficulties block progress, graphing a way ahead requests a nuanced and key methodology. This part investigates a far reaching guide for exploring the mind boggling territory of political stop, reestablishing vote based essentialness, and cultivating a more responsive and comprehensive administration. From institutional changes to cultivating political exchange, the accompanying methodologies offer a multi-layered structure for pioneers trying to break liberated from stagnation and revive the popularity based soul.

1. **Institutional Changes: Rehashing the Apparatus of Administration**

   Tending to political impasse requires a basic assessment and, when important, a reevaluation of institutional systems. Pioneers should assess constituent frameworks, administrative strategies, and regulatory designs to recognize and correct foundational defects that add to gridlock. Relative portrayal, for example, can upgrade inclusivity, while smoothed out official cycles can assist independent direction.

   Institutional changes ought to be driven by a pledge to straightforwardness, responsibility, and responsiveness. Pioneers who champion such changes signal a takeoff from conventional power elements and a certified obligation to recharging popularity based processes. By connecting with specialists, requesting public information, and teaming up across partisan loyalties, pioneers can produce an agreement on institutional changes that lay the foundation for breaking the stop.

102

"

2. **Political Discourse and Bipartisanship: Crossing over Partitions for Shared conviction**

   Breaking political gridlock requires a shift from fierce governmental issues to useful exchange. Pioneers should focus on bipartisanship, participating in open and earnest discussions across partisan divisions. Laying out systems for organized political discourse, like bipartisan councils or public gatherings, can make spaces for authentic commitment and the distinguishing proof of shared conviction.

   Bipartisanship expects pioneers to transcend philosophical contrasts and focus on the aggregate interest over hardliner increases. Pioneers who effectively look for cooperation signal a pledge to solidarity, encouraging a climate where compromise is seen as a strength as opposed to a shortcoming. Through supported exchange, pioneers can construct trust, destroy settled in places, and develop a political culture that values collaboration.

3. **Resident Strengthening: From Onlookers to Dynamic Members**

   Reestablishing majority rule imperativeness requires a change in outlook in the job of residents — from latent onlookers to dynamic members. Pioneers should put resources into systems that engage residents to assume a functioning part in administration. This includes casting a ballot in races as well as participating in participatory dynamic cycles, official Q&A events, and local area drives.

   Resident strengthening remains closely connected with straightforward and open administration. Pioneers who give clear data, energize public info, and effectively include residents in dynamic encourage a feeling of pride and obligation among the general population. From nearby administration designs to public policymaking, resident strengthening turns into an impetus for breaking political gridlock by enhancing different voices and guaranteeing strategies line up with the necessities and yearnings of individuals.

4. **Social Union Drives: Recuperating Divisions In the public eye**

   Political impasses frequently reflect cultural divisions, gaining social union drives basic for headway. Pioneers should effectively attempt to connect separates, resolving issues connected with character, financial variations, and social contrasts. Drives that advance inclusivity, exchange among networks, and social comprehension can add to recuperating cultural breaks.

   Reality and Compromise Commission in South Africa fills in as a powerful illustration of a social union drive. By recognizing verifiable treacheries, cultivating exchange, and advancing compromise, the commission assumed a critical part in modifying a cracked society. Pioneers looking to break political stop should perceive the interconnectedness of political and social issues, effectively attempting to establish a climate where variety is commended, and divisions are patched.

5. **Hostile to Defilement Measures: Reestablishing Public Trust**

Debasement disintegrates public confidence in political establishments and compounds political impasses. Pioneers should focus on enemy of debasement measures to reestablish trust in the majority rule process. This includes reinforcing oversight systems, carrying out straightforward monetary practices, and considering those took part in degenerate exercises responsible.

Systematizing hostile to debasement estimates flags a pledge to moral administration, encouraging a climate where residents accept their chiefs act in the public interest. Pioneers should work as a team with common society associations, global bodies, and free guard dogs to guarantee the viability of hostile to defilement drives. By uncovering debasement, pioneers can prepare for reestablished trust in political cycles and break the halt brought about by doubt and thwarted expectation.

6. **Media Education and Dependable Reporting: Exploring the Data Scene**

In the time of data, exploring the perplexing territory of political stop requires an educated populace. Pioneers should focus on media education drives to furnish residents with the abilities to fundamentally assess data sources and observe reality from fiction. Mindful news-casting assumes a critical part in this undertaking, as media associations should maintain editorial morals and give precise, impartial data.

Pioneers can team up with news sources, instructive foundations, and innovation organizations to advance media proficiency. By encouraging a climate where residents are prepared to explore the data scene, pioneers add to an additional educated and connected with public. Thus, this helps break the gridlock by moderating the impact of deception and cultivating a culture of decisive reasoning.

7. **Worldwide Collaboration: Drawing Motivation from Worldwide Models**

Breaking political halt can profit from drawing motivation from effective global models. Pioneers ought to effectively look for bits of knowledge from nations that have explored comparative difficulties and executed successful changes. Worldwide collaboration can include associations with associations like the Unified Countries, sharing prescribed procedures, and taking part in conciliatory drives that cultivate joint effort.

Scandinavian nations, famous for their elevated degrees of social trust and viable administration, act as instances of effective models. Pioneers can concentrate on the components that add to their political solidness, social attachment, and financial flourishing. By gaining from worldwide victories and adjusting demonstrated methodologies, pioneers can diagram a way ahead that reverberates with the exceptional setting of their country.

8. Future-Arranged Approach Arranging: Expecting Difficulties and Embracing Development

Breaking political stop requests a forward-looking way to deal with strategy arranging. Pioneers should expect future difficulties, from mechanical disturbances to natural emergencies, and proactively foster arrangements that address arising issues. Embracing development in administration, including the utilization of innovation and information driven direction, guarantees that political cycles stay versatile and responsive.

Situation arranging, an essential foreknowledge method, can assist pioneers with expecting likely prospects and devise strategies that are strong to vulnerabilities. By drawing in with specialists, think tanks, and futurists, pioneers can develop a policymaking climate that is dynamic and fit for breaking liberated from stagnation. Future-arranged strategy arranging cultivates a climate where pioneers are not simply responding to prompt difficulties yet are effectively forming the direction of their country.

A Comprehensive Methodology for Vote based Recharging

Diagramming a way ahead despite political impasse requests a comprehensive and interconnected approach that tends to the main drivers of stop while reviving the majority rule soul. From institutional changes to resident strengthening, social union drives, and future-situated strategy arranging, the systems illustrated in this outline give pioneers a complete structure for breaking liberated from stagnation.

The outcome of these systems lies in their mix and versatility to the remarkable setting of every country. Pioneers should perceive the interchange between political, social, and institutional elements, effectively looking for cooperative arrangements that reverberate with the assorted necessities of their constituents.

Chasing vote based recharging, pioneers become planners of progress, guiding their countries towards a future described by responsiveness, inclusivity, and a restored feeling of municipal commitment. As they explore the complicated landscape of political impasse, pioneers embracing this all encompassing methodology contribute not exclusively to breaking stop yet in addition to establishing the groundwork for a versatile and dynamic majority rule government.

7.1 Proposals for political and institutional reforms to mitigate gridlock.

Proposition for Political and Institutional Changes: Alleviating Gridlock and Upgrading Administration

Notwithstanding persevering political gridlock, described by dug in partisanship and institutional dormancy, proposition for complete political and institutional changes are vital. This part frames a bunch of nuanced and key changes pointed toward relieving gridlock, encouraging collaboration, and improving the general viability of administration. From electing framework upgrades to regulative procedural changes, the accompanying proposition comprise a guide for pioneers looking to break liberated from the shackles of stop and advance a more unique political scene.

1. **Constituent Framework Redesign: Cultivating Corresponding Portrayal**

   A central change to moderate gridlock includes upgrading the discretionary framework, moving towards corresponding portrayal. Dissimilar to first-past-the-post frameworks, which frequently bring about champ brings home all the glory situations, corresponding portrayal guarantees that the sythesis of the authoritative body reflects the appropriation of votes. This supports multi-party portrayal and decreases the probability of a solitary party ruling the political scene.

   Nations like Germany and New Zealand, with their blended part relative portrayal frameworks, embody how this approach can cultivate joint effort and decrease polarization. By boosting gatherings to cooperate and addressing a more different scope of perspectives, corresponding portrayal can separate the twofold idea of governmental issues, relieving gridlock and encouraging a more helpful world of politics.

2. **Positioned Decision Casting a ballot: Empowering Agreement Up-and-comers**

   Positioned decision casting a ballot presents one more encouraging change to lighten gridlock by empowering possibility to speak to a more extensive range of citizens. In this framework, electors rank competitors arranged by inclination, and in the event that no up-and-comer gets a greater part in the primary round, the up-and-comer with the least votes is disposed of, and their votes are reallocated in light of citizens' subsequent options. This interaction go on until a competitor accomplishes a larger part.

   Positioned decision casting a ballot reduces the "least damaging options" dynamic frequently connected with first-past-the-post frameworks, advancing the appointment of agreement competitors who can collect help past their nearby base. This change limits the potential for outrageous partisanship, empowering lawmakers to embrace more moderate places that reverberate with a more extensive supporters.

3. **Redistricting Change: Shortening Manipulating**

   Manipulating, the act of controlling discretionary locale limits to lean toward one ideological group, contributes altogether to political polarization and gridlock. Improving the redistricting system to guarantee decency and forestall sectarian control is vital for alleviating gridlock. Free, non-sectarian redistricting commissions can assume a significant part in creating locale that mirror the genuine socioeconomics and political inclinations of a district.

   States like California and Arizona have carried out free redistricting commissions, lessening the effect of manipulating. By laying out straightforward and unprejudiced instruments for redrawing constituent guides, pioneers can cultivate serious decisions, deter outrageous partisanship, and make a more delegate political scene.

4. **Official Technique Updates: Smoothing out Navigation**

The complexities of authoritative techniques frequently add to gridlock, with delays, cloture rules, and complex advisory group structures blocking productive independent direction. Corrections to official techniques can smooth out processes, speed up direction, and advance a more cooperative climate. Carrying out stricter timetables for specific authoritative cycles, lessening the edge for cloture, and improving on advisory group structures are expected changes.

The reception of a "most optimized plan of attack" instrument, where certain issues considered urgent for the country's prosperity are exposed to a sped up regulative interaction, can get through gridlock on basic matters. By decisively modifying official methods, pioneers can establish a climate helpful for split the difference and agreement building.

5. **Bipartisan Advisory groups: Working with Cross-Party Coordinated effort**

To relieve gridlock and advance bipartisan collaboration, pioneers can lay out particular bipartisan advisory groups entrusted with resolving explicit issues. These boards of trustees would involve individuals from various gatherings, cultivating joint effort, and empowering administrators to settle on some shared interest on key approach matters. Bipartisan boards of trustees can possibly get through sectarian partitions and create extensive, agreement driven arrangements.

The outcome of this approach is apparent in the U.S. Senate's Select Council on Knowledge, where individuals from the two players cooperate on issues of public safety. By extending the utilization of bipartisan panels to address a more extensive scope of issues, pioneers can make devoted spaces for cross-party cooperation, diminishing the effect of gridlock on basic strategy regions.

6. **Required Consultation Meetings: Empowering Top to bottom Conversations**

Gridlock frequently comes from an absence of inside and out conversations on basic issues. Pioneers can present obligatory consideration meetings as a feature of the regulative cycle, expecting legislators to take part in exhaustive discussions and investigate different points of view prior to deciding on proposed regulation. Consideration meetings, worked with by specialists or impartial arbitrators, give an open door to administrators to dive into the subtleties of intricate issues.

Nations like Switzerland use a deliberative model through residents' gather-

. ings, taking into consideration far reaching conversations before significant choices. By integrating deliberative components into official cycles, pioneers can encourage a more educated and smart dynamic climate, lessening the penchant for gridlock in light of shallow or philosophical contemplations.

7. **Reinforcing Governing rules: Saving Popularity based Values**

While gridlock can block quick direction, protecting the governing rules inborn in just systems is fundamental. Pioneers should work out some kind of harmony between relieving gridlock and guaranteeing that power isn't amassed in that frame of mind of government. Fortifying governing rules includes supporting the autonomy of the legal executive, engaging administrative bodies, and maintaining the job of the council in considering the chief responsible.

Nations like India, with a hearty legal executive that practices legal survey, feature the significance of keeping up with governing rules. Pioneers can carry out changes that support the independence of oversight foundations, building up equitable qualities while moderating gridlock in a way predictable with sacred standards.

8. **Public Supporting of Decisions: Shortening Unique Interest Impact**

Decreasing the impact of unique interests and advancing fair rivalry can add to breaking gridlock. Pioneers can advocate for public funding of decisions, restricting the dependence on confidential gifts and reducing the influence of strong vested parties. Public supporting guarantees that up-and-comers have equivalent admittance to assets, advancing a more level battleground.

Nations like Canada and Sweden have effectively carried out open supporting frameworks, controling the effect of cash in legislative issues. By supporting this change, pioneers signal a promise to lessening the unjustifiable impact of exceptional interests, cultivating a political scene where choices are driven by the requirements and wants of the electorate as opposed to the monetary sponsorship of strong substances.

An All encompassing Way to deal with Change

Moderating gridlock through political and institutional changes requests an all encompassing and nuanced approach that tends to the main drivers of stop while saving the center precepts of vote based administration. From electing framework updates to regulative method modifications, the proposition illustrated in this part give pioneers an extensive tool stash for restoring popularity based processes.

The outcome of these changes lies in their versatility to the exceptional settings of various countries. Pioneers should cautiously consider the interchange between different proposed changes, perceiving that a blend of changes might be important to accomplish significant outcomes. By embracing these changes, pioneers can establish a climate where joint effort and compromise are supported as well as fundamental for the compelling working of majority rule foundations. In breaking liberated from gridlock, pioneers become designers of a more responsive, comprehensive, and dynamic political scene, establishing the groundwork for a versatile and flourishing vote based system.

7.2 Successful policy changes that have addressed root causes of political stalemate.

Fruitful Arrangement Changes Tending to the Underlying drivers of Political Impasse: Illustrations from Worldwide Encounters

In the midst of the difficulties of political impasse, there exist motivating instances of fruitful arrangement changes that have really tended to main drivers and revived administration. This section investigates assorted cases from around the reality where creative arrangements have gotten through gridlock, cultivated joint effort, and resolved fundamental issues. From constituent changes to institutional developments, the accompanying cases give significant illustrations to pioneers looking to explore political halts and advance compelling administration.

1. **Ireland's Residents' Gathering: Comprehensive Independent direction**

   In the consequence of the financial emergency, Ireland confronted political impasse on issues of social significance, especially concerning established and moral matters. The public authority answered by laying out the Residents' Get together in 2016, a deliberative body containing haphazardly chosen residents entrusted with resolving explicit issues. The gathering assumed a crucial part in depoliticizing hostile subjects, giving suggestions on disruptive issues, for example, early termination and environmental change.

   The outcome of Ireland's Residents' Gathering lies in its obligation to inclusivity and thought. By including customary residents in dynamic cycles, the get together guaranteed a variety of viewpoints that rose above political partitions. The model grandstands the capability of comprehensive systems for breaking political impasse, cultivating agreement, and reestablishing public confidence in the popularity based process.

2. **Germany's Blended Part Relative Portrayal: Cultivating Alliance Building**

   Germany's discretionary framework, known as blended part relative portrayal, has been instrumental in moderating political impasse and advancing alliance building. Dissimilar to first-past-the-post frameworks, this model joins supporters based portrayal with relative portrayal. It urges gatherings to team up and frame alliances, as single-party strength is more outlandish. Germany's experience exhibits the way in which discretionary framework changes can encourage a more cooperative world of politics, getting through the gridlock related with champ brings home all the glory frameworks.

   The German model stresses the significance of relative portrayal in reflecting assorted citizen inclinations. By keeping away from a severe two-party framework, the electing framework boosts gatherings to settle on some mutual interest and team up. Pioneers wrestling with political stop can draw motivation from Germany's methodology, perceiving that constituent changes can assume a vital part in molding the elements of administration.

3. **New Zealand's Blended Part Corresponding Framework: Empowering Agreement Legislative issues**

New Zealand's reception of the blended part relative (MMP) framework in 1996 denoted a critical takeoff from its past first-past-the-post framework. The MMP framework, like Germany's, plans to guarantee that the creation of the council mirrors the extent of votes each party gets. This move was a reaction to saw imbalances in the past framework, where parties with huge famous help yet less body electorate wins were underrepresented.

The MMP framework in New Zealand has supported agreement legislative issues by requiring alliance state run administrations. Ideological groups should arrange and team up to shape a larger part in the parliament, deterring champ brings home all the glory mindsets. This shift has added to a more comprehensive political scene, separating conventional obstructions and cultivating a culture of give and take and collaboration.

4. **The Reasonable Consideration Act (ACA) in the US: Steady Change In the midst of Sectarian Separation**

The section of the Reasonable Consideration Act (ACA) in the US in 2010 stands apart as an uncommon illustration of critical strategy change amidst profound hardliner divisions.

The ACA planned to resolve longstanding issues in the American medical care framework, growing admittance to medical services through a blend of Medicaid development, health care coverage commercial centers, and customer securities. The progress of the ACA in exploring political gridlock mirrors the significance of gradual change and bipartisan split the difference.

While the ACA was met with savage hardliner resistance, its prosperity lay in the key sequencing of changes and think twice about key arrangements. The regulation, however not without defects, addresses a takeoff from the customary way of thinking that significant strategy changes are unimaginable in profoundly separated political environments. The ACA experience highlights the potential for nuanced, bit by bit ways to deal with address complex issues, offering experiences for pioneers wrestling with political gridlock.

5. **South Africa's Reality and Compromise Commission: Mending Divisions**

In the outcome of politically-sanctioned racial segregation, South Africa confronted the great undertaking of accommodating a profoundly separated society. Reality and Compromise Commission (TRC), laid out in 1995, assumed a urgent part in tending to verifiable treacheries and cultivating public recuperating. The TRC gave a stage to casualties and culprits to share their accounts, adding to an aggregate comprehension of the past while conceding pardon to the individuals who admitted their violations.

South Africa's TRC represents the groundbreaking force of truth-telling and compromise processes. By recognizing verifiable wrongs and encouraging a public discourse, the TRC added to social union and relieved the potential for persevering through political impasse. Pioneers wrestling with well established divisions can draw examples from South Africa's methodology, perceiving the significance of truth, pardoning, and aggregate recuperating in getting through political halt.

6. **Scotland's Devolution: Fitting Administration to Provincial Requirements**

Scotland's excursion towards devolution, coming full circle in the foundation of the Scottish Parliament in 1999, fills in as a model for tending to provincial differences and moderating political impasse. Devolution conceded Scotland critical controls over homegrown issues, considering approaches custom-made to the particular requirements and inclinations of the Scottish public. This approach has encouraged a more responsive and comprehensive administration structure, lessening strains and likely gridlock.

The outcome of Scotland's devolution lies in its acknowledgment of territorial independence and the capacity to pursue choices nearer to the impacted networks. By decentralizing power and fitting administration to local subtleties, Scotland has relieved political strains and shown the viability of declined administration structures in tending to political impasse.

7. **Colombia's International agreement with FARC: Settling Firmly established Struggle**

Colombia's international agreement with the Progressive Military of Colombia (FARC) in 2016 denoted the finish of an extended clash that had endured for over fifty years. The harmony interaction, intervened with global help, resolved firmly established issues of political prohibition, social imbalance, and country improvement. The understanding included arrangements for FARC's demobilization, their progress into political life, and responsibilities to address underlying drivers of the contention.

The Colombian international agreement shows the potential for settling political impasse through thorough harmony processes. By resolving fundamental primary issues and cultivating comprehensive discourse, pioneers can change settled in clashes into open doors for enduring compromise. The Colombian case underscores the significance of global intercession and a guarantee to tending to main drivers in accomplishing economical harmony.

8. Taiwan's Progress to A majority rule government: Exploring Philosophical Partitions

Taiwan's change to a majority rules government in the late twentieth century gives bits of knowledge into beating political impasse with regards to philosophical partitions. The shift from a dictator system to a multi-party a majority rule government included cautious talks, political changes, and a guarantee to cultivating vote based values. Taiwan's experience shows the significance of building spans between various political philosophies to lay out a steady and working popularity based framework.

Key components of Taiwan's prosperity incorporate a continuous progress, political changes that obliged different points of view, and a guarantee to popularity based standards. The country's capacity to explore philosophical partitions and construct an agreement around just administration fills in as a significant model for pioneers wrestling with settled in political polarization.

Core values for Compelling Change

The fruitful approach changes framed above offer core values for pioneers looking to address the underlying drivers of political impasse. Inclusivity, gradual change, and a promise to resolving fundamental issues are repeating themes winding through these cases. By drawing examples from worldwide encounters, pioneers can explore the complicated landscape of political stop, cultivating coordinated effort, and rejuvenating administration. The groundbreaking force of these strategy changes lies in their nearby effect as well as in their capability to shape a more responsive, comprehensive, and dynamic political scene to serve residents and the soundness of majority rule establishments.

7.3 Vision for a more collaborative and effective political landscape, and the potential impact on alleviating human suffering.

A Dream for a Cooperative and Powerful Political Scene: Reducing Human Torment and Cultivating Comprehensive Administration

In imagining a political scene portrayed by joint effort, viability, and inclusivity, the likely effect on reducing human enduring turns into a convincing story. This vision rises above the regular comprehension of legislative issues as a landmark of clashing belief systems, offering a guide for pioneers to develop a more responsive and empathetic administration model. From encouraging social union to executing creative strategies, the accompanying investigation frames a dream for a political scene that puts the prosperity of residents at its center.

1. Encouraging Social Attachment: Building Scaffolds Across Partitions

At the core of a cooperative political scene is the obligation to cultivating social union. Pioneers imagine a general public where residents, regardless of their different foundations, feel a feeling of having a place and common perspective. By building spans across philosophical, social, and financial partitions, political pioneers can establish a climate where exchange replaces dissension and understanding supplants ill will.

This vision accentuates the significance of pioneers effectively captivating with networks, paying attention to different points of view, and recognizing the wealth that variety brings to the political talk. Drives that advance social trade, local area exchanges, and comprehensive portrayal in dynamic cycles add to the embroidered artwork of social union. A cooperative political scene perceives the strength got from solidarity and effectively attempts to patch cultural fractures, in this way lightening the human experiencing that frequently emerges divisions inside networks.

2. **Comprehensive Direction: Engaging Each Voice**

In the imagined political scene, navigation is a really comprehensive cycle that engages each voice, guaranteeing that the worries of underestimated and weak populaces are heard as well as effectively tended to. Pioneers focus on making instruments like resident gatherings, participatory planning, and comprehensive policymaking discussions. These stages act as channels for direct resident inclusion, permitting people from varying backgrounds to straightforwardly add to the molding of strategies that influence them.

This obligation to comprehensive navigation reaches out to embracing variety inside legislative designs. A different portrayal of orientation, nationality, and financial foundations inside political establishments guarantees a variety of viewpoints, enhancing the policymaking system. This inclusivity isn't just emblematic however is reflected in strategies that elevate underestimated networks, address foundational imbalances, and effectively make progress toward the improvement, everything being equal.

3. **Creative Strategies Tending to Main drivers: An All encompassing Methodology**

A cooperative and viable political scene is described by a promise to tending to the main drivers of cultural difficulties as opposed to simply treating side effects. Pioneers imagine strategies that adopt an all encompassing strategy, understanding that interconnected issues require exhaustive arrangements. For instance, in handling destitution, pioneers wouldn't just zero in on direct financial mediations yet additionally address factors like schooling, medical care, and foundational obstructions to social versatility.

In this vision, imaginative strategies flourish, driven by proof based navigation and a promise to continuous assessment and variation. Pioneers bridle the force of innovation, information, and interdisciplinary coordinated effort to plan and execute arrangements that are receptive to the advancing requirements of their networks. Such arrangements act as vehicles for positive change, breaking the pattern of human affliction and encouraging a climate where residents can flourish.

4. **Fortifying Medical care Situation: A General Right**

   Inside the cooperative political scene, medical services isn't treated as an honor yet as a central basic liberty. Pioneers perceive the significance of strong, available, and fair medical care frameworks that abandon nobody. General medical services turns into a foundation, guaranteeing that each resident approaches fundamental clinical benefits without the weight of devastating monetary expenses.

   Interests in preventive medical care, psychological wellness administrations, and local area based care add to a thorough and comprehensive way to deal with prosperity. Pioneers focus on wellbeing schooling, advancing sound ways of life and proactive measures to forestall sicknesses. By setting the wellbeing and prosperity of residents at the front, a cooperative political scene turns into an impetus for easing human misery and guaranteeing that nobody faces outlandish boundaries to medical services.

5. **Ecological Stewardship: Feasible Strategies for People in the future**

   A visionary political scene places natural stewardship at its center, perceiving the interconnectedness of environmental wellbeing and human prosperity. Pioneers focus on economical strategies that address environmental change, safeguard biodiversity, and advance capable asset the board. In this vision, legislatures effectively partake in global endeavors to battle worldwide natural difficulties, understanding that the outcomes of biological corruption are felt by networks around the world.

   Strategies advancing clean energy, protection, and dependable metropolitan arranging add to a reasonable future. Pioneers imagine a shift away from momentary increases that hurt the climate toward long haul systems that focus on the prosperity of people in the future. By embracing earth cognizant strategies, a cooperative political scene turns into a power for moderating the effects of environmental change and saving the planet to serve all.

6. **Training as Strengthening: A Guarantee to Deep rooted Learning**

   In the imagined political scene, training is seen as an integral asset for strengthening and cultural advancement. Pioneers focus on a complete school system that goes past scholastic figuring out how to incorporate decisive reasoning, imagination, and versatility. This remembers speculations for youth instruction, professional preparation, and advanced education availability.

   Also, the obligation to instruction reaches out past conventional foundations. Long lasting learning is empowered, with pioneers supporting drives that make constant schooling available to people at each phase of life. By encouraging a general public that qualities and puts resources into schooling, pioneers add to breaking the pattern of destitution, enabling residents to seek after satisfying professions, and cultivating a culture of development and progress.

7. **Social Security Nets: A Sympathetic Way to deal with Emergency**

A cooperative political scene puts an exceptional on empathy, especially during seasons of emergency. Pioneers focus on laying out and reinforcing social wellbeing nets that give a support to residents confronting monetary difficulties, cataclysmic events, or wellbeing emergencies. Hearty social security nets incorporate joblessness benefits, lodging help, and medical care during crises. This vision perceives that cultural prosperity is interconnected and that supporting people during testing times isn't just an ethical objective yet additionally an interest in the strength and solidness of networks. Pioneers effectively draw in with social help associations, NGOs, and local area pioneers to guarantee that the most weak citizenry are secured and elevated during seasons of emergency.

8. **Innovation for Comprehensive Turn of events: Crossing over the Advanced Gap**

In the cooperative political scene, innovation is saddled as a power for comprehensive improvement as opposed to compounding existing variations. Pioneers focus on crossing over the computerized partition, guaranteeing that mechanical headways benefit all residents. Drives to improve advanced proficiency, grow admittance to the web, and influence innovation for distant training and medical services become fundamental parts of administration.

Besides, pioneers effectively manage and direct mechanical advancement to forestall manhandles and guarantee moral practices. Arrangements focus on information protection, network safety, and mindful utilization of arising advancements. By embracing innovation as an instrument for comprehensive turn of events, pioneers add to diminishing differences, encouraging development, and establishing a climate where the advantages of progress are shared evenhandedly.

9. **Worldwide Collaboration for Worldwide Difficulties: A Unified Front**

The cooperative political scene stretches out past public boundaries, with pioneers effectively captivating in worldwide collaboration to address worldwide difficulties. Whether handling pandemics, exile emergencies, or transnational dangers, pioneers imagine a reality where countries work cooperatively, pooling assets and skill to track down arrangements.

This vision underscores strategy, discourse, and organizations as fundamental devices for exploring the intricacies of a globalized world. Pioneers focus on maintaining worldwide standards, deals, and arrangements, perceiving the interconnectedness of human torment and progress on a worldwide scale. By encouraging a unified front despite shared difficulties, pioneers add to a more steady, secure, and merciful world.

A Humane and Versatile Future

The vision for a cooperative and powerful political scene is grounded in the conviction that legislative issues can be a power for good, effectively adding to the easing of human misery and the upgrade of cultural prosperity. Pioneers, directed by standards of inclusivity, development, and empathy, can possibly change the political talk and develop an administration model that focuses on the necessities of residents.

This vision reaches out past the bounds of appointive cycles, underscoring the drawn out effect of approaches and the heritage that pioneers can leave for people in the future. It requires a pledge to values that rise above hardliner partitions, putting the benefit of all at the front of navigation. The possible effect on easing human enduring is significant, as this cooperative political scene turns into an impetus for positive change, strength despite challenges, and an encouraging sign for an additional sympathetic and fair future.

7.4 Call to action for individuals, communities, and political leaders to work towards breaking the gridlock.

A Source of inspiration: Breaking the Gridlock for a Flourishing Future

Despite tenacious political gridlock, the source of inspiration resonates for political pioneers as well as for people and networks to pursue breaking the stagnation and encouraging a more responsive and comprehensive administration by and large. The way to a flourishing future requires a coordinated exertion from all partners, rising above conventional partitions and embracing a common obligation to the standards of joint effort, sympathy, and extraordinary change.

People: Problem solvers in Their People group

The source of inspiration starts with people perceiving their organization as influencers inside their networks. Every resident holds the ability to impact the political scene through dynamic commitment, informed navigation, and a pledge to values that focus on the benefit of all. People are encouraged to:

Remain Educated and Locked in: Effectively search out different wellsprings of data, basically assess viewpoints, and remain informed about nearby and world-wide issues. Participate in local area gatherings, official Q&A events, and take part in conversations that add to a very much educated populace.

Vote Dependably: Exercise the option to cast a ballot capably by exploring up-and-comers, grasping their positions, and settling on informed decisions. Perceive the effect of neighborhood races on local area prosperity and effectively partake in the popularity based process.

Advance Common Talk: Cultivate a culture of common talk and deferential exchange inside networks. Support open discussions that span philosophical holes, perceiving the worth of different viewpoints in molding comprehensive arrangements.

Volunteer and Team up: Add to local area prosperity by chipping in time and abilities. Team up with neighborhood associations, non-benefits, and metro gatherings to resolve major problems and make positive change at the grassroots level.

Consider Pioneers Responsible: Consider chose authorities responsible for their activities, request straightforwardness, and effectively partake in responsibility components. Advocate for approaches that focus on the requirements of the local area and challenge pioneers to rise above hardliner partitions.

Networks: Supporting Inclusivity and Strength

Networks assume a crucial part in breaking the gridlock by cultivating a feeling of having a place, inclusivity, and versatility. The source of inspiration for networks includes:

Advancing Inclusivity: Embrace variety inside the local area and effectively pursue establishing a comprehensive climate where each voice is heard and esteemed. Perceive the strength that comes from a variety of points of view and encounters.

Building Social Union: Put resources into drives that form social attachment, encourage trust, and fortify local area bonds. Support social trade programs, local area occasions, and activities that unite occupants and separate social obstructions.

Resolving Neighborhood Issues: Distinguish and resolve nearby issues co-operatively. Urge people group individuals to effectively partake in dynamic cycles that influence the area, and backer for approaches that address the novel difficulties looked by the local area.

Enabling the Helpless: Focus on drives that engage weak populaces inside the local area. Advocate for social wellbeing nets, support neighborhood noble cause, and work towards addressing foundational imbalances that add to human anguish.

Instructing and Assembling: Advance training and mindfulness inside the local area on basic issues. Activate people group individuals to partake in city exercises, participate in exchange, and team up on projects that improve the general prosperity of the local area.

Political Pioneers: Spearheading Extraordinary Change

For political pioneers, the source of inspiration reaches out past constituent vows to a pledge to extraordinary change that rises above sectarian lines. Pioneers are encouraged to:

Focus on Bipartisanship: Effectively look for potential open doors for bipartisan coordinated effort, perceiving that viable administration requires participation across partisan principals. Lay out bipartisan advisory groups and gatherings that address central points of contention confronting the country.

Take part in Straightforward Administration: Focus on straightforwardness in dynamic cycles. Discuss transparently with the general population, give clear clarifications to strategy choices, and effectively look for input from residents to guarantee a more comprehensive and participatory administration model.

Put resources into Municipal Schooling: Perceive the significance of community training in encouraging an educated and drew in populace. Put resources into instructive projects that advance metro education, decisive reasoning, and a profound comprehension of popularity based standards.

Champion Constituent Changes: Supporter for electing changes that advance reasonableness, inclusivity, and a more delegate political scene. Think about choices like relative portrayal, positioned decision casting a ballot, and redistricting changes to upgrade the vote based process.

Focus on Long haul Vision: Move past transient political gains and focus on a drawn out vision that focuses on the prosperity of residents and the supportability of networks. Carry out arrangements that address underlying drivers as opposed to only treating side effects.

Aggregate Activity: Producing an Eventual fate of Coordinated effort and Progress

The source of inspiration finishes in the acknowledgment that breaking the gridlock requires aggregate activity — people, networks, and political pioneers working together as one towards a future portrayed by joint effort, sympathy, and progress. This aggregate activity includes:

Making Stages for Discourse: Lay out stages that work with open exchange between people, networks, and political pioneers. Municipal events, local area gatherings, and advanced stages can act as spaces for useful discussions that rise above political partitions.

Supporting Grassroots Developments: Recognize and uphold grassroots developments that promoter for positive change. These developments frequently act as impetuses for breaking the gridlock by bringing issues to light, preparing networks, and constraining pioneers to resolve major problems.

Putting resources into Schooling: Focus on instruction as a foundation of extraordinary change. Put resources into instructive drives that cultivate decisive reasoning, city commitment, and a profound comprehension of the obligations that accompany living in a popularity based society.

Embracing Mechanical Advancement: Bridle the force of innovation to interface networks, work with coordinated effort, and upgrade city commitment. Influence computerized stages for data sharing, participatory administration, and activating aggregate activity towards shared objectives.

Supporting for Underlying Changes: Supporter for primary changes that address the main drivers of political gridlock. This incorporates constituent changes, institutional changes, and approaches that improve the flexibility and versatility of political frameworks.

Advancing Compassion and Grasping: Cultivate a culture of sympathy and understanding inside society. Urge people to effectively pay attention to different points of view, challenge previously established inclinations, and fabricate extensions of understanding that rise above political, social, and financial contrasts.

Observing Examples of overcoming adversity: Feature and celebrate examples of overcoming adversity where cooperative endeavors have prompted positive change. These accounts act as motivation and models for replication, displaying that breaking the gridlock isn't just imaginable yet reachable through purposeful endeavors.

An Aggregate Obligation to a More promising time to come

In noting the source of inspiration, people, networks, and political pioneers add to the co-making of a future described by joint effort, inclusivity, and progress. Breaking the gridlock is certainly not a single undertaking yet an aggregate obligation to building a general public that focuses on the prosperity of its residents and encourages a climate where the standards of a majority rule government are maintained.

As people participate in informed municipal cooperation, networks fabricate scaffolds of understanding and backing, and political pioneers champion groundbreaking change, the vision of a flourishing future turns into a substantial reality.

This aggregate responsibility rises above the difficulties of the present, producing a way towards a more splendid, stronger, and comprehensive future for a long time into the future. In this common excursion, breaking the gridlock turns into an image of trust and a demonstration of the extraordinary force of aggregate activity.

7.5 Vision for a future where political processes contribute to the well-being of society rather than perpetuating human suffering.

A Dream for a Future: Political Cycles Catalyzing Cultural Prosperity

In imagining a future where political cycles are systems of administration as well as impetuses for cultural prosperity, a significant shift is expected in the manner in which we conceptualize and rehearse legislative issues. This vision rises above the conventional jobs of political foundations, putting the accentuation soundly on their capacity to contribute decidedly to the general government assistance of society. A call for extraordinary change tends to the underlying drivers of human misery and use political cycles as instruments of progress, empathy, and strength.

1. **Comprehensive Prosperity at the Center: A Change in outlook in Administration**

   The vision starts with a change in perspective that places all encompassing prosperity at the center of administration. Political cycles are reconceptualized not just as frameworks for overseeing assets and authorizing regulations yet as powerful systems intended to upgrade the personal satisfaction for all residents. This shift includes a reconsideration of strategy needs, perceiving that cultural prosperity incorporates financial pointers as well as variables like psychological well-being, ecological supportability, and social union.

In this vision, political pioneers work with a guarantee to the thorough government assistance of their constituents. Strategies are made with a profound comprehension of the interconnectedness of different parts of prosperity, tending to quick worries as well as laying the basis for maintainable success. The measurements of achievement for political cycles stretch out past Gross domestic product development to incorporate marks of satisfaction, value, and natural maintainability.

2. **Comprehensive Direction: Intensifying Assorted Voices**

At the core of the imagined future is a guarantee to comprehensive navigation. Political cycles become stages where different voices are heard as well as effectively searched out and enhanced. Pioneers perceive that genuine portrayal goes past segment checkboxes to envelop a certified comprehension of the horde points of view inside society.

This inclusivity is reflected in arrangements that address the exceptional requirements of minimized networks, it is abandoned to guarantee that nobody. Dynamic cycles are straightforward, open, and effectively include residents in molding the strategies that straightforwardly influence their lives. In this vision, the political scene turns into an embroidery of voices, mirroring the lavishness of human encounters and encouraging a feeling of having a place for all.

3. **Sympathetic Administration: Focusing on the Defenseless**

What's in store imagines a type of administration that is on a very basic level humane, focusing on the necessities of the most weak citizenry. Political pioneers work with compassion, effectively looking for answers for reduce human misery and address foundational imbalances. Strategies are created with an emphasis on friendly wellbeing nets, reasonable medical services, and backing for those confronting monetary difficulties.

The vision reaches out past momentary help to the execution of primary changes that destroy obstructions to prosperity. Pioneers effectively draw in with the encounters of minimized networks, recognizing verifiable treacheries and making progress toward reparative strategies that encourage a more impartial and just society.

4. **Reasonable Turn of events: Natural Obligation**

A future where political cycles add to cultural prosperity is innately interwoven with natural obligation. Pioneers perceive the earnestness of tending to environmental change, protecting biodiversity, and guaranteeing the supportability of regular assets. Political cycles become instruments for making and carrying out strategies that focus on ecological protection and environment versatility.

This vision sees the reception of clean energy drives, protection endeavors, and worldwide participation to handle worldwide natural difficulties. Approaches are made with a comprehension that the prosperity of society is naturally connected to the wellbeing of the planet. A promise to supportable improvement turns into a core value, guaranteeing that progress doesn't come to the detriment of people in the future.

5. **Training as Strengthening: Sustaining Informed Residents**

   In the imagined future, schooling is situated as an incredible asset for strengthening and cultural advancement. Political cycles focus on interests in schooling that go past scholastic figuring out how to encourage decisive reasoning, imagination, and metro commitment. The objective isn't simply to create gifted laborers yet educated and dynamic residents who contribute seriously to the majority rule process.

   Pioneers perceive the significance of available and evenhanded instruction, guaranteeing that each person, paying little heed to foundation, has the chance to arrive at their maximum capacity. The educational program mirrors a guarantee to variety, inclusivity, and a profound comprehension of popularity based standards. The schooling system turns into a foundation for supporting a general public of educated, drew in, and sympathetic residents.

6. **Mechanical Advancement for Social Great: Connecting Partitions**

   Later on vision, mechanical development is outfit as a power for social great, effectively crossing over partitions instead of compounding them. Political cycles embrace innovation to improve correspondence, work with community support, and address cultural difficulties. The computerized partition is effectively spanned, guaranteeing that mechanical headways benefit all residents, remembering those for underserved networks.

   Pioneers effectively manage and direct mechanical advancement to forestall mishandles and guarantee moral practices. Approaches focus on information protection, network safety, and dependable utilization of arising innovations. The computerized scene turns into an instrument for inclusivity, interfacing networks, encouraging cooperation, and enhancing the aggregate voice for positive change.

7. **Compromise and Worldwide Collaboration: A Unified Mankind**

   What's in store imagines political cycles as components for compromise and worldwide collaboration. Pioneers effectively participate in strategic endeavors to determine clashes, perceiving the interconnectedness of human experiencing on a worldwide scale. Political organizations become facilitators of worldwide participation, pooling assets and ability to address shared difficulties, for example, pandemics, exile emergencies, and transnational dangers.

In this vision, countries move past thin personal responsibility to embrace a feeling of shared mankind. Deals, arrangements, and strategic endeavors are driven by a guarantee to general basic liberties, nobility, and the aggregate prosperity of the worldwide local area. The political scene turns into a phase for building spans, encouraging comprehension, and pursuing a more amicable world.

8. **Public-Private Associations: Amplifying Assets for Prosperity**

What's to come sees a consistent cooperation between the general population and confidential areas, expanding assets for cultural prosperity. Political cycles effectively empower public-private organizations that influence the qualities of the two areas to address complex difficulties. Corporate obligation goes past net revenues to incorporate a promise to social and natural effect.

Pioneers effectively draw in with organizations to adjust financial exercises to cultural prosperity. Arrangements boost moral strategic policies, corporate social obligation, and interests in local area improvement. The collaboration among public and confidential substances turns into a main thrust for positive change, with a common obligation to cultural prosperity.

A Prospering Embroidery of Prosperity

The vision for a future where political cycles add to cultural prosperity is one of significant change and deliberate administration. It is a future where the intrinsic capability of political organizations to shape positive results is completely understood. The imagined scene is portrayed by inclusivity, sympathy, and a comprehensive comprehension of the variables that add to human prospering.

This future is definitely not a far off perfect world however an unmistakable objective that can be effectively sought after through purposeful strategy decisions, social movements, and aggregate endeavors. It requires political pioneers to embrace another worldview of administration, people to effectively take part in municipal life, and networks to encourage a feeling of having a place and common perspective. Together, these partners add to the co-making of a prospering embroidery of prosperity, where political cycles become a main impetus for a general public that flourishes with sympathy, manageability, and progress.